OMAHA
FOOD

RACHEL P. GRACE

OMAHA FOOD

BIGGER THAN BEEF

AMERICAN PALATE

Published by American Palate
A Division of The History Press
Charleston, SC
www.historypress.net

First published 2015

Manufactured in the United States

ISBN 978.1.46711.781.4

Library of Congress Control Number: 2015948835

Notice: The information in this book is true and complete to the best of our knowledge. It is offered without guarantee on the part of the author or The History Press. The author and The History Press disclaim all liability in connection with the use of this book.

CONTENTS

ACKNOWLEDGEMENTS

This project is the culmination of five years of a highly immersive, at times obsessive, experience with Omaha food that all started when I moved here in 2010. Conversations with new friends would most often turn to food; they'd immediately scribble out the names of their favorite places on bar napkins, insisting I had to try them. And so I did, fascinated by the level of persuasion that was unrivaled by any other city I had lived in before. Before long, I was going out to eat nearly every day trying to keep up with the recommendations, and people would check back with me, asking what I had thought. The semi-genius idea for a food blog was birthed out of necessity to keep track of my opinions—that, and a love of writing. At that point in time, there weren't any other active Omaha food blogs.

It would likely have not gone much further than that had it not been for the early supporters, those who sat around with me patiently—and sometimes impatiently—waiting to eat while I found just the right angle with my iPhone. Without a doubt, it was the enthusiasm of my original champions that motivated me to push forward. You know who you are.

I've been genuinely touched by the level of support given by a number of busy restaurant owners who didn't even bat an eye at the prospect of helping me out: Robert Tim Peffer at Sgt. Peffer's, Jeannie Ohira and Joe Pittack at Ted & Wally's, Paul Urban and Jessica Joyce Urban at Block 16, Lou Marcuzzo at Louie M's and Bryce Coulton of the French Bulldog, to name a few. In addition, the chefs and artisans who provided recipes for these pages are my heroes.

ACKNOWLEDGEMENTS

Thank you to Jon Hustead for coaching me on photography, and extra special thanks for believing that I could do it in the first place. I am indebted to Jon, as well as the other photographers who loaned their work for this project: Alexander Rock, Bill Sitzmann, Colin Conces, Dillon Gitano and Mark Swanson. Thanks also to the team at The New BLK for lending their constant opinions about restaurants. You're all a bunch of experts.

This book would have definitely been lacking something had it not been for Jessica Luna, who brought me up to speed on everything I needed to know about being a real native Omahan. She even let me borrow her mother and grandmother!

I selfishly convinced my sister, Lydia Catone, to move to Omaha just as this project was kicking off. She was a wonderful research companion and feedback provider, and I was extremely happy to have her be a part of it firsthand. And there is no doubt in my mind that I wouldn't have made it to the finish line without the support of Shane Bainbridge, who calmly reminded me why I was doing this in the first place as often as needed. He was my main connector, moderator and motivator—not to mention illustrator. (And he was forced to enjoy many nights out without me while I stayed home and worked, bless his heart.)

It's been clear for some time that Omaha food deserves a lot more attention than it's historically gotten, from residents and nonresidents alike. I'm thrilled to have had the chance to tell at least a part of that wonderful story. Thank you to Becky LeJeune and Artie Crisp at The History Press for making that possible.

No small thanks, either, to the guy who accidentally slammed his oafish body into me at the Sydney one night and broke my finger. While it forced me to lay off the guitar for a while, I could still type on a keyboard. I took this as a sign that it was time to act and write the book I had wanted to write for some time.

This is a city filled with incredible energy right now. Let's make the most of it.

INTRODUCTION

There are a lot of people in the United States who can't pick out Omaha on a map. I know because I used to be one of them. From Los Angeles to New York, Portland to Miami, sea to shining sea, a lot of fellow Americans couldn't care less about where Omaha is, generally speaking. Mention Omaha's food scene, and they start to glaze over. The perception that Nebraska is nothing but cornfields is alive and well, and the struggle to convince people otherwise is real.

In an attempt to win them over, I'll sometimes throw out to a jaded New Yorker that our airport only takes a few minutes to pass through security, which is pretty awesome. That is, until I remember that it's actually just an air*field*, with no international destinations. They'll often ask if Omaha has a lot of chain restaurants, to which I reply, "…sort of." What, are there no Olive Gardens east of the Mississippi? Sure, a 1993 book of reviews published by the *Omaha World-Herald*, the city's leading paper, included an Olive Garden review alongside real, locally owned, noteworthy restaurants, but so what? It's not like they reviewed T.G.I. Friday's and Chili's, too. (Except they did.)[1]

That was 1993, and this is today. The chain restaurant flak we give ourselves can go away now. Long before the national chains arrived, Omaha had an absolutely thriving restaurant scene.

Take the menu from 1944 seen on the next page, for example. I, personally, would love to have tried Baked Oma-Ham with French Fried Potatoes for fifty cents. Or perhaps the Genuine Castle Spaghetti, the recipe for which was

Above and opposite: Menu from the Hotel Castle. *Courtesy of Lou Marcuzzo.*

"procured from the Castle of Count Belvidere." It was likely over this very menu, in fact, at the Hotel Castle downtown, that the Omaha Restaurant Association was formed. Its founders, a group of seven early Omaha restaurateurs, had a lot of great eateries on their hands that they felt they needed to promote.[2] If I could fossilize any single moment in Omaha restaurant history, it would be that: a bunch of suits sitting around a table over their prime rib and braised ox joints, yammering on about how great the food is. It sounds suspiciously familiar.

Omaha is, and always has been, a food town by every generally accepted criteria—it just flew under the national radar for a while. If you're looking for chef-driven restaurants churning out new ideas, we've got that. If specialty eateries are your favorite fad du jour, then boy do we have something for you. With dozens of international cuisines represented in every capacity, from the strip mall hole-in-the-wall to the high-end dining destination, we've got that market covered, too.

And then there's the beefy reputation we couldn't live down even if we wanted to. (We don't.) On a recent trip to one of Omaha's famous, classic steakhouses, the power of search engine optimization had led one lone young working lad on a business trip to the table next to me. He was from Ohio (I know where that is) and had consulted Google about where he "could get a good steak" because "when in Omaha that's what you do." He was surprised to hear of other, non-steakhouse restaurants. I began to explain, and continued after he had stopped listening,

---

When in Des Moines—HOTEL RANDOLPH
THURSDAY JULY 20, 1944

LUNCHEONS
For Today

Soups   Juices
Old Fashioned Navy Bean 15c
Chicken Noodle Soup 15c
Orange, Tomato or Grapefruit Juice 15c
Crisp Celery Hearts 20c

✱ 50c ✱
BAKED OMA-HAM
French Fried Potatoes
Garden Fresh Cole Slaw
Rolls & Butter
✱ ✱

✱ 40c ✱
Hot Sirloin of Beef Sandwich.
Mashed Potatoes & Gravy
✱ ✱
Hot Ham Sandwich
Mashed Potatoes & Gravy
✱ ✱
Hot Pork Sandwich
Mashed Potatoes & Gravy
✱ ✱

30c GRILL SPECIAL 30c
Goose Liver Sausage Sandwich
Potato Salad
Radish - Dill Pickle
Coffee
✱ ✱

✱ SEA FOOD ✱
Fresh New Orleans Shrimp, a la Creole . 50c
Fried Channel Catfish, Butter Sauce . . 75c
Fried Filet of Lemon Sole, Tartar Sauce 40c
French Fried Potatoes, Combination Salad,
New Orleans Shrimp, on Ice 50c
Rolls & Butter   Coffee, or Tea.

✱ SUMMER SUGGESTIONS ✱
Roast Prime Rib of Beef 75c
Roast Loin of Pork 70c
Sliced Breast of Turkey 85c
(with above cold plate orders)
Potato Salad   Sliced Tomato   Pickle
Rolls & Butter
Choice of Beverage—Milk 5c Extra

No. 1 55c
Northern Channel Catfish, Saute, Meniere,
French Fried Potatoes,   Combination Salad,
Castle Rolls & Butter,   Coffee or Tea (hot or iced)

No. 2 50c
Ripe Tomato, Stuffed with Tuna Fish Salad,
Potato Salad,   Dill Pickle,   Radish,
Castle Rolls & Butter,   Coffee or Tea (hot or iced)

No. 3 45c
Braised Ox-Joints, Printaniere,
Whipped Potatoes,   Combination Salad,
Castle Rolls & Butter,   Coffee or Tea (hot or iced)

No. 4 45c
Boiled Fresh Spare-Ribs, Sauerkraut,
Boiled Potato,   Jello,
Castle Rolls & Butter,   Coffee or Tea (hot or iced)

No. 5 40c
Fricassee of Veal, Vegetables,
Whipped Potatoes,   Buttered Noodles,
Castle Rolls & Butter,   Coffee or Tea (hot or iced)

No 6 35c
Stuffed Bell Pepper, Meat Sauce,
Whipped Potatoes,   Cole Slaw,
Castle Rolls & Butter,   Coffee or Tea (hot or iced)

No. 7 30c
Golden Brown Corn Fritters,
Maple Syrup,
Coffee or Tea (hot or iced)

No. 8 25c
Soup of the Day,
Choice of our Home-Made Pies,   Coffee.

MILK 5c WITH ABOVE LUNCHEONS
DESSERTS FOR TODAY
Chilled Watermelon or Cantaloupe 20c
Vanilla, Chocolate Ice Cream or Sherbet 15c
Assorted Pies (Made by our own Baker - Every Morning) . . . 10c

---

Soups   Juices
Soup of the Day 15c   Chicken Broth with Noodles 15c
Orange, Grapefruit or Tomato Juice 15c

COCKTAILS
FRESH JUMBO SHRIMP COCKTAIL 35c
Castle Cocktail Sauce Saltine Wafers
FRUIT COCKTAIL, SUPREME 25c

REFRESHING SALADS
'THE ELITE' SALAD BOWL 50c
Mixed greens, Tomato and julienne of chicken,
topped with delicious Chef's dressing.
FRESH SHRIMP SALAD, ... 60c
Sliced Tomatoes, Hard Boiled Egg, Finger Sandwiches.
HENRI'S SPECIAL SALAD BOWL 45c
with His Famous Dressing, Rolls.

SANDWICHES
Plain or Toasted
Roast Beef . . . . 25c   Roast Pork 25c
American Cheese . . . . . 15c   Denver 25c
Fried Egg . . . . 15c   Grilled Ham 25c
Baked Ham . . . . 25c   Ham and Egg 30c
Bacon and Tomato . . . . 25c   Corned Beef 20c
Ham Salad . . . . 20c   Chicken Salad Sandwich . 30c
Ox-Tongue . . . . 25c   Chicken Sandwich 40c
Egg Salad . . . . 20c   Special Club Sandwich . . 50c

-SUGGESTIONS-
Calf's Liver, Saute, Bacon . 50c   Pan-Fried Pork Chops . . . 60c
Broiled Club Steak 65c

Combination Salad, 1,000 Island Dressing,
French Fried Potatoes, Rolls, Coffee, Tea

HARD ROLLS-CHOICE OF DRINK - MILK 5c EXTRA

Ham and Eggs or Bacon and Eggs 50c
With two slices Golden Brown Toast and Long Branch Potatoes.
Nebraska Products at their best.

Genuine Castle Spaghetti 40c
With rich Meat Sauce and Parmesan Cheese, Hard Rolls or
Wafers. Recipe procured from the Castle of Count Belvidere.

All prices are our ceiling prices, or below. By O. P. A.
regulation, our ceilings are based on our highest
prices from April 4th to 10th, 1943. Our menus or price
lists for that week are available for your inspection.

Fountain Menu
✱ ✱ ✱

COLD DRINKS
Lemonade, plain 10c
Egg Lemonade 15c

Orange or Two Tone Juice 15c
Tomato or Kraut Juice, Small 15c
Grape Juice 15c
Cola 10c
Root Beer 10c
Fresh Limeade 10c
Grapefruit Juice 15c
Fruit Phosphate or Plain 10c

MALTED MILKS
Malted Milk 20c
Egg Malted Milk 25c
Milk Shake 15c
Egg Milk Shake 25c

SUNDAES
Butterscotch 15c
Hot Fudge 20c
Chocolate 15c
Assorted Fruit 20c
Chocolate-Marshmallow 20c
Marshmallow 15c

Castle Hotel Special 20c

SODAS
Chocolate 15c
Vanilla 15c

Root Beer Float 15c
Orange 15c
Lemon 15c

Cherry 15c
Ice Cream or Sherbet 15c

FEATURES
That Famous Jumbo Chocolate Soda . . 20c

HOT DRINKS
Hot Chocolate and Wafers 10c
Hot Chocolate 10c
Coffee, Pot . . 10c Tea, Pot 10c
Assorted Soups . 15c (Cream of Tomato) 20c
"We use only Standard Pasteurized Milk"

that Omaha has been quietly turning out some of the best cuisine in the Midwest for some time. We don't jump at trends; we're just more selective, eschewing the boring ones and embracing the best. It's a cluster of old-school favorites mingling with the contemporary, and it would be good if we could outgrow the steak reputation to allow some other qualities to shine, even if just for a minute.

The fact is that Omaha is constantly changing. When I think of all the restaurants I go back to again and again, most of them weren't open yet in 2010. Just a short time later, I'm faced with the issue of having way too much to talk about in this book—a good problem to have, really. I encountered enough material to easily fill ten books. And I'm finding that Omaha isn't all that different from other cities undergoing a similar period of restaurant renaissance. It could be that we are coming full circle, arriving at a point close to where we started in 1944, when everything was new and exciting and people talked about food so much they started restaurant associations. Yes, that sounds about right.

This story of Omaha food opens with an account of the early days—a city that prospered with the livestock industry of the 1950s. It works its way through changing neighborhoods and changing tastes, an over-the-top passion for pizza and a strong appreciation for good beer. It's the story of why the dishes we hold near and dear will forever have a special place next to the cultural demolition of our collective comfort zone. There's a whole wide country out there; sometimes being smack-dab in the middle gives you the best view. Omahans can, after all, name other cities on the map.

Chapter 1

THE BEEF STATE, ALWAYS AND FOREVER

November 21, 1955: an unseasonably mild Monday morning that was otherwise unremarkable. Overnight, the *Omaha World-Herald* presses chugged away on their series of inked letters, as they'd been doing for seventy years. Just before dawn, young paper delivery boys chucked their inventory into the Missouri and went back to bed—or I like to think they usually did that, like little rebels.

Surely, it was business as usual. Golden retrievers bouncily fetched their masters' papers, and wives across the city poured coffee with one hand while vacuuming with another, one leg curled behind them like sexy homemaker gymnasts. Husbands flipped open the thin folded paper like they did every morning, educating themselves on current events in Omaha and beyond. To some, the front-cover headline that morning probably felt as though Christmas had come early that year.

Omaha had been founded in the 1850s on the premise that it would become something big, and city advocates had been jockeying for quite some time for the official title of "Largest Livestock Market in the World." I like to think of the city's founders as something like old-school A&R people, but instead of sniffing out the next YouTube sensation to dominate the pop culture world, they were looking for the perfect land on which to build a city that would become a solid center of commerce in the young nation's growing midsection. And like most good Americans, they were impatient. This wasn't some long-winded, far-off future plan they hoped their grandchildren would benefit from. The men and women who first came over from Iowa, put a

Omaha claiming the largest cattle market a few years early in 1951 on the L Street Viaduct. *Courtesy of the Durham Museum and KM3TV.*

stake in the ground and said, "This is Omaha," were definitely looking to make some fast mo-ney-ney.[3]

They would do that, they thought, with the railroads and the promise of abundant land for newcomers. They hyped the crap out of the place. An 1873 pamphlet authored by the alluringly poetic state superintendent of immigration named J.H. Noteware says it all:

Nebraska is the last agricultural State in America offering cheap and good Homesteads to the landless. Every one [sic] knows that there are large countries north and west of Nebraska yet unsettled; but they are either mineral, lumber or grazing countries, which cannot be occupied by a numerous and prosperous and independent population; this fact is becoming well known.

Nebraska is the only remaining State wholly and richly agricultural and pastoral; "where millions of acres are almost donated to the brave pioneers of the world, by the generous Government of America."

In five years every square mile in the east half of the State will all be actually occupied and farmed; while every township in the west half of the State will be filled with tens of thousands of cattle and sheep. On every hill will wave the golden harvest or feed the quiet herd; in every vale will nestle among trees and vines the peaceful cottage; along every principal valley the iron horse will draw his rolling palaces.

The hum of machinery, mingled with the din of tramping feet and rattling wheels, and cheery voice of men and fowls and beasts will fill the air and forever annul the silence of nature.[4]

I suppose one could say that things were looking quite promising in Nebraska, and Omaha in particular. The vision of the area as a prime place to monetize cattle was definitely there from the start, but it wasn't until about ten years later, in 1883, that a posse of local businessmen made it top priority. For who could look at Chicago's prosperous stockyards and not want a piece of that action? They truly believed that they could do it better, too: better grazing space, better transportation and a better location closer to actual ranchers and cattlemen than what Chi-Town had.[5] Much like the record company exec who first heard Taylor Swift in the back of a tiny Nashville nightclub, this was the start of something magical, a recipe for juicy, sizzling success. Cha-ching.

This group of investors—including those with such locally recognizable surnames as Creighton, Paxton, Woolworth and Kountze—took meticulous steps to ensure the success of their brainchild. They started offering attractive financial bonuses to lure Chicagoan packinghouse owners down to their city on the Missouri, which should have been a no-brainer. If someone offered me $100,000 (which is something like $3 million in today's dollars) to relocate to Omaha from Chicago, I don't think I would have hesitated either. To be more precise, this was all going down in what was actually South Omaha at the time, a separate entity that wouldn't become part of Omaha proper through annexation until 1915. By 1889, the South Omaha Stockyards had a capacity of ten thousand cattle, twenty thousand hogs, five thousand sheep and five hundred horses and mules, not to mention roughly ten thousand humans in the adjacent residences, all built in the span of five years. A major boom even by nineteenth-century pioneer standards, this substantial growth earned South Omaha the nickname the "Magic City."[6]

Not so magical was what actually went on down at the yards, unless you're super into animal slaughter. At its height in the early 1950s, pen after pen of cattle lined an area more than fifty square blocks organized by narrow alleys, where buyers and cattlemen would haggle prices by the pound and then finish their transactions in the ten-story Livestock Exchange Building that loomed over the whole operation. About seventeen packing plants kept the demand fulfilled and more than ten thousand people employed. It wasn't

Inside the cattle auction, 1945. *Courtesy of the Durham Museum.*

really the place for queasy stomachs or sensitive noses, but it was for those who liked having a steady job, whether that was on the kill floors, in the coolers or in the specialty cut rooms.[7]

In 1955, when Omaha surpassed Chicago as the world's largest stockyards, that dad reading the newspaper that Fido brought in had about a 50 percent chance of being employed in the livestock industry in some shape or form.[8] I'm sure on that day everyone took some comfort in knowing they were part of something big.

Because "Kansas City Steaks" Doesn't Have the Same Ring

Thanks for sitting through the "Rise of the Omaha Stockyards" story. You might be thinking, *Great, I'm so glad that these truckloads of cattle passing through town brought remarkable prosperity to the city, attracting tens of thousands of workers and billions of dollars over time. I promise to thank the stockyards every day as I drive through the city on my way to work, since these roads probably wouldn't even be here if*

Omaha didn't start right off the bat as such a flourishing, wondrous place with plentiful employment opportunities and bountiful food to eat. If it weren't for the stockyards, I'd probably have been born in, like, Council Bluffs or something. Yeesh.

I don't think anyone can say for sure what would have happened if Omaha didn't have the stockyards. It's hard to say if five Fortune 500 companies still would have headquartered here and if the solid financial foundation would have made Omaha relatively protected against national recessions. But a few things are for certain: without the stockyards, the alluring aroma of cattle poo wouldn't occasionally waft up your nostrils on particularly windy afternoons on the southern side of town. Without the stockyards, there would not have been the acute demand for nearly as many butchers in town, those who found their calling carving up locally slaughtered meats to sell to Omaha's ever-growing, ever-hungry, hardworking population. In 1955, an impressive 6.4 million animals showed up with a one-way ticket from the prairie land in convoys of trucks hauling their product primarily from the west of the city. Then, from 1956 to 1965, just to remind the rest of the Midwest that it was the industry leader, Nebraska license plates even boasted the tagline "The Beef State."[9]

To be honest, though, Omaha at the time wasn't all that different from similar stockyards in other cities of the Heartland: Wichita, Chicago, Fort Worth and St. Louis all had impressive yards within their city limits; experienced butchers in their workforce; and ubiquitous beef dishes in their recipe collections. In her 2005 book *America's Historic Stockyards: Livestock Hotels*, author J'Nell L. Pate only bothered to devote six and a half pages to Omaha's story. And "steak dinners" were en vogue all across the nation—an invitation for which often signifying just how serious your courtship with Jimmy was about to become. (Cough cough.)

The question has to be raised: if cattle farming and, consequently, beef eating was as American as apple pie, how did Omaha get to be the lucky one to run off with the title of unofficial steak capital of the country? I think the answer lies in the success of one business in particular, begun by an industrious man named J.J. Simon, who arrived in 1898 with his son B.A. a long way from home in Riga, Latvia. A butcher by trade, in 1917 he took over an ailing storefront already bearing the name Table Supply Co., which seemed like a fine name for the business of selling cuts of meat to the public, so he kept it. But not before scraping together some limited funds to amend the signage, nudging the "Co." to the right and inserting the word "Meat." And thus, Table Supply Meat Company was born. He did a fine business in town before seizing the opportunity in the late '40s to leverage Omaha's super good beef and sweet location on the Union Pacific Railroad.

For in these years right before travelers ditched their train passes in favor of their own Cadillacs and Impalas and Mustangs (and, in some cases, tickets for Braniff and Delta), rail car dining was huge. What you snacked on in between cities was an event in and of itself.

It should surprise no one that Table Supply Meat Company's scrumptious steaks were a huge hit. Diners from all corners of the country began inquiring about the origin of the juicy porterhouses on the plates before them so they could ask for it the next time around. They'd then go to their homes all

Workers pause for a photograph in the meat processing area at Table Supply Meat Company's first building, Seventeenth and Douglas Streets. *Courtesy of Omaha Steaks.*

Workers unloading the famous wet-aged steaks from a railroad car at Table Supply Meat Company. *Courtesy of Omaha Steaks.*

over the forty-eight contiguous states and surely have pleasant dreams about the steak from Omaha with impeccable marbling and tender yet flavorful qualities. Before long, requests for Omaha steaks were sweeping train cars across the Union Pacific.

The company grew steadily. As it built a new headquarters and expanded its consumer business, the time came for a rebrand in 1966. Table Supply went for something a little simpler that hadn't yet been trademarked by anyone, in honor of its top selling item: Omaha Steaks International. There might be something to having the right name after all.[10]

THE GOLDEN AGE OF STEAK

If this book were a movie, now would be the time for a fast-paced, feel-good montage with images of happy, smiling people grilling and eating steaks set to "What I Like About You." In it, a middle-aged, salt-and-pepper gentleman watches the grill with an all-knowing smile, a striped apron and a shiny pair of tongs, while his trophy wife looks on lustfully. Photogenic families of the "2.5 kids and a white picket fence" variety take pleasure in an afternoon picnic outdoors, replete with the splendor of steaks and sun. Two young couples enjoy a double date spent accidentally clinking each other's long forks in a quintessential early '70s beef tip fondue scene. Each cut of meat comes off as picturesque as the last, grill lines and all—garnished with a lush sprig of parsley, of course.

Such was the experience of paging through an Omaha Steaks mail-order catalogue circa 1972. With a keen sense for advertising—it ran its first ad in the *New Yorker* in '58 and has since become the longest-running advertiser in that publication—the company added home delivery to its services around the same time and complemented it with some pretty entertaining catalogues it sent out to thousands of potential customers, a relatively novel approach at the time. At the urging of J.J.'s grandson Lester, it also capitalized on

Department store window display, Omaha, 1937. *Courtesy of the Durham Museum.*

several key mid-twentieth-century inventions that would make mail-order perishables possible: Polystyrene shipping coolers, vacuum packaging and direct parcel shipping. The company's first toll-free 1-800 number was another exciting addition in 1975. And thus, when train travel went out of fashion, the company found a new way to solidify its mark and Omaha's culinary reputation nationwide at the same time. The early catalogues are peppered throughout with gushing testimonials backing up this claim. One of many gems, from a Mr. James C. Megraw in Drexel Hill, Pennsylvania, reads, "I have eaten in the best (and the worst) places in the 48 states. You have proven my belief that the people of Omaha know more about meat than anyone else in the world."

The sprawling, present-day headquarters of Omaha Steaks near 108th and O Streets does feel a bit like the command center for meat experts. It's there that I asked Todd Simon, senior vice-president and a fifth-generation family owner, to ponder the success of the company and the cornering of the mail-order meat market. "I think in a lot of ways my grandfather [Lester Simon] had an intuition around the fact that we had this geographical advantage," he told me. "Omaha was at the center of the beef industry at the time. It's the same way that people liked to eat lobsters from Maine, wine from Bordeaux, oranges from Florida. We offered something different and really used our location to our advantage."[11]

Although Omaha Steaks still supplies the beef to a loyal legion of local and regional restaurants, about 95 percent of the business today is straight to consumer. Its biggest markets are on the coasts, and it goes through 41 million pounds of dry ice annually getting the product to the people—just the single largest user of dry ice in North America, no big deal. I can attest that people from the coasts don't spend a ton of time with Omaha on the brain; when they do, quality steaks are mostly what they think of, and this has a lot to do with why.

The Smell of Money

While Omaha Steaks was gaining momentum as the premier delivered-to-your-door provider of steaks and chops in the country, one eatery in town had been serving the very population of workers that was doing all the heavy lifting all along. In a standalone building right on the edge of the stockyards at Twenty-seventh and L, Johnny's Café has been in operation since 1922.

Purchased from an existing business with the same name, the building began as a very noble eight-table establishment that expanded along with the stockyards, tacking on a new addition every few years to accommodate the growing numbers of workers that would line up for beef sandwiches at lunchtime.

The man who started it all was Frank Kawa, a Polish immigrant who arrived in the United States with not much more than the company of a few cousins sometime in the early twentieth century. There aren't too many people left who might remember the Prohibition era firsthand, so it was news to the rest of the Kawa family when they were researching their ancestry and unearthed some *Omaha World-Herald* reports from the time that suggested Frank wasn't the most law-abiding citizen of the land. He swore up and down that he sold only soda pop beverages, but he was still arrested for the production and sale of "real beer" at the height of Prohibition madness in 1928. Despite Frank's arrest and time in jail served, the restaurant continued on, and over the years he even started answering to the name "Johnny." The lawbreaking eventually became the stuff of legends, taking a backseat to the restaurant's acclaim.[12] But when I say Frank at least looks like a gangster, with his floating face adorning many iterations of the menu throughout the years, I mean that in the most endearing way possible.

If you can just pretend for a minute that you're a stockyards worker wearing manure-covered boots and carrying an empty stomach in search of a quick meal—and didn't feel like going home to eat—you would understand how and why Johnny's became so popular. In the early days, the clientele was not a very sanitary bunch, but hey, a guy's gotta eat. To mentally deal with the unsavory perfume of poo wafting around all the time, the Johnny's team—and those associated with the stockyards by and large—likened the smell to that of money. For wherever there were plentiful cattle, there was a profit to be made.

I am told that it wasn't uncommon to have cows chilling directly outside the back door. Opaque coffee cups masked the fact that whiskey was routinely drank throughout the day. The lighting came from gas lanterns, and the floors generally had a coat of sawdust at all times. It wasn't until the '40s and '50s that Johnny's started refining itself into a proper restaurant. This is when the favorite dishes we know and love were developed, and after that, there was no turning back. The two co-owners today, sisters Sally Kawa and Kari Kawa Harding, are the third generation behind their father, Jack, and grandfather Frank. They tell me that while the menu has changed over time to accommodate food trends (anyone remember the assault on dietary fat in the late '80s and early '90s that made every menu suddenly include a chicken and seafood dish?), the recipes themselves are by and large the originals. And that right there is why the French onion soup is to die for—it tastes pure, uncomplicated. You get the feeling that the stock, made from the most flavorful bones they could find, has been simmering for days. Instead of masking the flavors behind a potpourri of herbs like some contemporary recipes do, this one's all about simple perfection: are the onions chopped properly, is the cheese freshly shredded and is the wedge of bread the right size?

My casual request for the soup recipe for publication within this book was politely declined, although I think what they really wanted to say was, "I'd tell you, but then I'd have to kill you." Another rather emotional dish is the cottage cheese spread, which since the '50s has been served complimentary along with a basket of white dinner rolls and cracker packets. Not the most advantageous of freebies from a food cost perspective, the rich dairy spread was temporarily eradicated sometime in the '80s, only to be met with "mutiny" by the regulars, as I'm told. It's a wonderful thing to savor before prime rib or New York strip. The steaks, by the way, are aged on-site, as they always have been, and recipes continue to be made entirely from scratch.[13] This includes the glorious onion rings—some of the best in town. And to separate itself from the Italian steakhouse competition, Johnny's sometimes offers a pierogi appetizer on special, a nod to the Polish heritage.

In Alexander Payne's 2002 film *About Schmidt*, Jack Nicholson and June Squibb drive in total silence to Nicholson's character's retirement banquet at Johnny's. Movie critics described the scenery as "not terribly ritzy," which isn't inaccurate.[14] A trip to Johnny's seems much less about the extravagance of eating a nice steak; since it's been around for so long, the focus is really more about enjoying classic recipes in an iconic setting that makes you feel like you're also ingesting just a little bit of uncensored history. Behold the nearly one hundred years' worth of menus on the lobby wall on the way out and giggle at the notion that frogs' legs had their time in the spotlight at one point. Enjoy the low tabletops; the high ceilings; the deep, rich colors; and the sizable photographic mural of cattle on the wall. Sink in with a few rounds of Manhattans and feel as though you are a tiny speck in a larger-than-life world and, at the same time, that you're royalty worthy of the finest red meat in the country.

OMAHA FOOD

DANCING THE NIGHT AWAY

From across the table at Gorat's Steak House, my friend Jessica eyed my plate of food that had just arrived, checking for accuracies. I ordered the same thing she did: one petit filet mignon, medium rare; side of hash browns, well done; and a side of mostaccioli with red sauce. "You have to get the bite of filet and potato and a little bit of sauce on the fork all at once," she instructed me as the first-timer at the table. "Don't worry about eating the pasta; it's more about getting some of that sauce on there." This is the restaurant she's been dining at with her family virtually her entire life, the place for family reunions, First Holy Communions, anniversaries and birthdays. She might as well have followed up the eating instructions with one of those animalistic grunts of culinary pleasure and a slight head nod side to side, but I did that for her. She was right. That's one heck of a bite.

I was there with Jessica's mother, Barbara, and Barbara's mother, Lois. Barbara told me about how she once learned the best way to tenderize steaks from the former owner of Gorat's, a man named Louis but known as "Pal." His method, according to her, was to wrap up the steak as tightly as possible in cheesecloth and give it a few good whacks against the tabletop. This way, the steak mechanically tenderizes while maintaining the integrity of its shape and thickness. After a few martinis, Pal's alleged method sounded like pure genius to me.

Gorat's is an Omaha original steakhouse, one of only a few left. It opened in 1944 in a converted house on a road we'd hardly recognize as busy Center Street near Forty-ninth Avenue today. Lois, at ninety years young, told me that one of the reasons she and her family came to Gorat's so often was because they'd get the best of everything. I suspect she's not the only Omahan who feels that way. Jessica shared her memories of one waitress in particular, a charming woman with a bun permanently fashioned on top of her head. She told me of her affinity for the strange-sounding dish of fried parsley—how it's reminiscent of fried pickles and not as weird as it sounds. Sadly, I didn't get to try it that day; when ownership changed hands a few years ago, it was removed from the menu. Our server informed us that they still occasionally make it upon request but that all the fresh parsley had already been chopped for the busy upcoming weekend. Indeed, every dish emerged from the kitchen garnished with a rather heavy hand of the green stuff, which I found pleasantly old-school. Saturday night dancing is still a thing here, too, with regular live acts performing on the curved stage on the bar side of the building.

If billionaire stalking sounds fun to you, and if you stick around long enough, you are likely to witness Warren Buffett dining here. I hear it's not totally uncommon to see the likes of Bill Gates along with Buffett in the table next to you. When prompted, many Omahans can recite Buffett's typical order, which is collectively creepy of us but kind of endearing, too: it's the T-bone steak, cooked rare, with a double order of hash browns (he must not care for the pasta) and a Cherry Coke. It's not surprising that most, if not all, of Berkshire Hathaway shareholders have followed Buffett here during one of the annual shareholder meeting weekends, held in the spring.

From an outsider's perspective, it's important to note two things: one, contrary to what might be expected, "Gorat" does not rhyme with "Borat," the pseudo–Central Asian film character from Kazakhstan. Rather, the stress is on the second syllable (gor-*ahtz*), and it even starts to meld into a single syllable coming off the tongue of those who have been saying it forever (*gratz*). Secondly, Buffett's regular patronization may seem like the hallmark of the Gorat's identity. But to Jessica's family and those alike, Gorat's is all about the traditions, whether that's an after-meal stroll across the dance floor or ordering a plate of onion rings before even being seated. Similar to the experience at Johnny's, Gorat's takes us back to a time of simplicity, when recipes called for three or four ingredients at most and folks were content with spending their evening in one place over a three-hour dinner. Personally, I feel I could get used to that kind of living.

Play On, Pete

In the mid-2010s, a countdown of sorts started forming in Omaha's collective psyche: it was of the number of classic steakhouses that are still functioning. With every closure announcement—and it seemed there was a new one every few years—the feeling was always bittersweet. No one wanted to see Caniglia's Venice Inn shutter, as it did in 2014, for example. The plot of land it used to sit on still feels weird to pass by. With every breaking news story of another closure, the general protocol for dealing with the pain kicks into action. There's always a public outcry first ("It's amazing they couldn't find a buyer to keep it going."), followed by evidence of self-disappointment and disgust ("What do you expect in an age when we order Jimmy John's online all the time?") and, finally, a celebration of the restaurant's life, much like the wake of a loved one. Folks share stories online of their own memories of

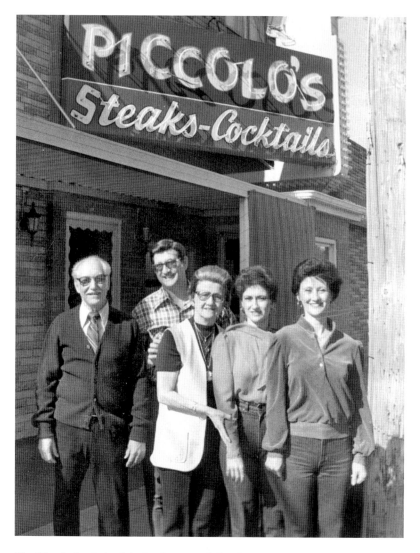

The Piccolo family back in the day, one of Omaha's restaurant greats. *Courtesy of Douglas County Historical Society.*

the subject in question ("I've been going there since I was seven years old."), and just like that, the big, imaginary ticker keeping track of the number of Omaha steakhouses flips to one number fewer.

One such story can be found about thirty blocks to the east of Gorat's at a spot called Piccolo Pete's Restaurant. I first learned of it from one rather gristly, looks-old-for-his-age regular at a local pub who claimed that it was the best steakhouse in town. The more I learned, the more I understood it to also have one of the richest restaurant histories I've ever known.

Similar to Johnny's, as well as Gorat's up until it was sold and a number of other restaurants we'll get into later, Piccolo's was a family operation. It was Joseph Piccolo who arrived from Sicily in 1909 and turned an old blacksmith shop into a grocery in 1922, the same year Frank Kawa opened Johnny's. Piccolo and his wife, Grace Caniglia, lived above the business in a vibrant neighborhood that bordered Omaha and South Omaha at the time; in more recent years, the area had changed a ton. Piccolo's didn't have any commercial neighbors and very few residential, so it's the iconic restaurant sign—a colorful glowing neon depicting a piccolo player—that dominated the view as you rolled south on Twentieth Street.

When that pesky Prohibition era ended in 1933, the Piccolos didn't waste any time turning their place into a beer garden. On that very first night when alcohol became legal, patrons spilled out onto the street and lined the block toasting their mugs of beer. Soon thereafter, a food menu was introduced, and the storied history of Piccolo Pete's Restaurant began.

As this was an Italian-style steakhouse, entrées were typically served with a golden disc of shredded, fried and salted potatoes known as hash browns and a separate side dish of mostaccioli that was mostly naked except for the sizable scoop of red sauce in the middle of it. Like Gorat's, Piccolo's was once a hot spot to show off your dance moves, under a large, elegant crystal ball hanging over spotless terrazzo floors.

Scott Sheehan, grandson of the original Piccolo, started up a food truck named after his uncle called Anthony Piccolo's Mobile Venue in 2014. Designed with elements of the original Piccolo's in mind—you will never see mostaccioli depicted this large on the nose of a truck anywhere else—he serves more abbreviated, hand-held versions of Italian steakhouse food, like prime dip sandwiches. It's nice to see a treasured Omaha steakhouse embrace something new. "This is the next generation," Scott told me.

Restaurant Roll Call

Oh but wait, there's more! Omaha is home to a handful of other classics, each one having earned a special place in people's hearts in different ways. If Jessica's family had a preference for Gorat's, there are others out there who adopted these as their go-to spots for family celebrations and special occasions. You never know if the day will come when one of these will send us into mourning by becoming another casualty of time; regardless, they've already earned themselves a spot in the annals of Omaha steakhouse greats.

The Drover

A regular on national "Best Of" lists, the Drover features Omaha's very first salad bar, initiated when the building was a franchise called the Cork and Cleaver. It was born in 1968 and, with all due respect, looks like it hasn't really been updated since then, from a culinary standpoint. Glistening ice cubes hold containers of cherry tomatoes, bacon bits, shredded carrots, standard croutons and Dorothy Lynch dressing (the recipe for which was first made in Nebraska), all meant to adorn your freshly chopped iceberg lettuce. The result is a little personalized masterpiece that you've gotten up out of your seat to create. It's a novel idea that might seem outmoded, but there's something sort of magical about the salad that keeps people flocking to it. The whiskey steak is the key item here that gets a fair amount of national attention, and for good reason: it's a fourteen-ounce New York strip that's been wet aged and then marinated in bourbon, soy sauce and garlic. It sure is a beaut, yielding perfect grill marks and an ever-so-slightly sweet finish.[15] The Drover's rendition of the Reuben sandwich, with tender slices of prime rib instead of the normal corned beef, is another original dish to try. Plus, it's super dark in there, for those times when "bad hair" and "hot date" fall on the same day.

Anthony's Steakhouse

Anthony's is the product of the long career of Tony Fucinaro, who founded the 120-seat dining room and 80-seat lounge in 1967.[16] From there, it kept growing and growing, into the 1,000-seat behemoth it is today located just off I-80 on Seventy-second Street. Its uber-expansive menu suggests a willingness to please and offers "something for everyone," and indeed Anthony's remains a popular location for banquets. It is perhaps best known today as "the one with the giant fiberglass steer on the roof," a sight that is not only memorable but also worthy of your best Omaha vacation Instagram. Fucinaro kept it really real, working hard for sixteen-hour days the majority of his tenure before dying at age eighty-two in 2013. It was just that important to him for customers to have that extra welcoming feel from the owner. Time will tell which direction Anthony's will head in, but for now, it remains an Omaha institution.

Cascio's Steakhouse

On a recent spring Saturday afternoon at 4:28 p.m., I witnessed an ancient couple walking rather adorably arm in arm up to Cascio's; it opens at 4:30 p.m. Such has been the sight since the restaurant started in 1946. This is yet another third-generation Italian steakhouse, and at 2,200 seats, it's by far the largest. It also has no problem filling those seats on a regular basis. Cascio's takes "from scratch" and "consistency" to the next level: the baker, chef and grill cook have been with the restaurant for twenty-five, thirty and forty years, respectively. Situated on the edge of the Little Italy neighborhood, this is an intense operation that functions like a well-oiled machine. Cascio's takes its marinara seriously, simmering it for seven hours each day. It also features an original-recipe pizza on the menu alongside the standards that you'd expect.

I felt compelled at first to poke fun at how the façade appears to be one of those Eastern Bloc–inspired, bare-bones deals with very few windows, but then I learned that this is actually the second Cascio's building. The first was destroyed by an arsonist in 1978, and it took two years to rebuild. The case went unsolved for twenty years. It wasn't until 1998 that the arsonist bragged to undercover investigators that he had entered through the building's roof in an attempt to rob the place, and when he couldn't get into the safe, he got angry and set the building aflame.[17] So, while the building might look a little "county jail chic" on the outside, it's what's on the inside that counts.

SURVIVAL OF THE TASTIEST

Cascio's is without a doubt one of the greats, but its physical enormity and wide-ranging menu go against the grain of incoming food trends, which opt for a more intimate, specialized approach. Before this, in the '70s, '80s and '90s, diners moved away from family-owned and instead gravitated toward the consistency and predictability of the chain restaurant experience. With

The late and great Marchio's Italian Café, a steakhouse favorite at Thirteenth and J Streets. *Courtesy of Douglas County Historical Society.*

that, Omaha lost some of its former greats that are still reflected on today, proving that adaptability is a wise trait to have in this business. There was Sam Nisi's Sparetime Café, Ross's Steak House, Al Caniglia's Top of the World, Mr. C's Steak House, Cantoni's, Trentino's, Angie's, Lucky's, Marchio's and, of course, the Original Caniglia's. All fell victim either to changing times or aging owners, whichever came first, and all are missed by their own little factions of fans. After all, these were the places where memories were made.

After restaurateur Gene Dunn purchased Gorat's in 2012, there were some changes, of course, and most of them any rational diner would agree were for the better, such as standard interior renovations and a few menu tweaks. Other details remained intact, like the wall of mirrors in the ladies' restroom—aka hours of amusement for my friend Jessica at age eight. And yet she and her family can tell that "it just feels different" than it did before. But if it weren't for Mr. Dunn, Gorat's might not be around any longer, period. We can then all agree that a slightly altered restaurant is better than no restaurant at all.

At the core of a successful restaurant is its devotion to the community that supports it. Omaha's classic steakhouses are certainly not epicenters of innovative plating, chef celebrity or Google-before-you-order-it ingredients. But the essence of what they offer to their patrons beyond what comes out of their kitchens—trust, longevity and a sense of community—can be a model for all of this century's wonderful new restaurants on the rise. And for that reason especially, these classics deserve a spot in your rotation.

The Industry Standard

If you've been to Omaha lately, you may have noticed that the massive stockyards are no longer. Just to maintain that irresistible cattle farm funk smell, there are still some successful meatpacking businesses in that same South Omaha area, but the actual yards closed up in 1999. In the late '60s, the meatpackers began doing business directly with the ranchers out where they were located on the prairies. In a time of increased mobility and improved communication, there just wasn't a need for the stockyards, which essentially acted as a middleman, any longer.

The city of Omaha on its own is no longer a major center of commerce for the beef industry, but if you look to the rest of the state, where one in four hamburgers in the nation has its origin, you can rest assured that "we still got it." In March 2014, Nebraska became the leader in the nation for cattle feeding, surpassing Texas with 2.46 million cattle on feed. As a throwback to this heritage, "The Beef State" license plates officially became available again in 2014 after forty-nine years on hiatus.[18]

Omaha is considerably distinct from the rest of the state in terms of landscape, socioeconomics, ethnic diversity and even politics. (The city, for example, possesses a single electoral college vote in the presidential election, which it famously offered to the Democratic ticket in 2008 while the rest of the state's electoral college votes went the Republican way.) But one thing Omaha does definitely have in common with the rest of Nebraska is its beefy heritage. This is particularly true when one considers the development of the Omaha restaurant scene as we know it, during which this highly available edible resource played a huge part. Nicole Jesse, co-owner of La Casa Pizzaria, once expressed her dismay at the short-lived steak menu the restaurant introduced in the 1970s: "At one point, because of the times, we had steaks, too. We eventually weaned those off."

It's not the '70s anymore, and while gourmet burgers are all the rage in Omaha, as they are across the country, beef dishes are more often sharing menu space not only with chicken, pork and seafood but also with duck, rabbit and a comfortable influx of vegetarian entrées. At the same time,

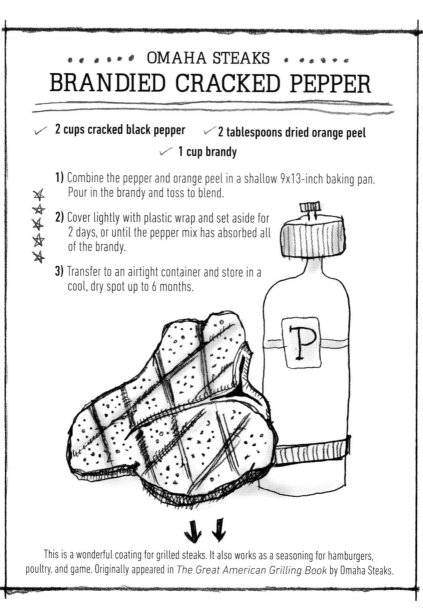

• • • • • OMAHA STEAKS • • • • •
BRANDIED CRACKED PEPPER

- 2 cups cracked black pepper
- 2 tablespoons dried orange peel
- 1 cup brandy

1) Combine the pepper and orange peel in a shallow 9x13-inch baking pan. Pour in the brandy and toss to blend.

2) Cover lightly with plastic wrap and set aside for 2 days, or until the pepper mix has absorbed all of the brandy.

3) Transfer to an airtight container and store in a cool, dry spot up to 6 months.

This is a wonderful coating for grilled steaks. It also works as a seasoning for hamburgers, poultry, and game. Originally appeared in *The Great American Grilling Book* by Omaha Steaks.

local chefs are exploring less common cuts and new preparations more and more. What better place than Omaha, Nebraska, to dig in on some tongue, cheek or sweetbreads? As you're about to see, the Beef State legacy still rings true for Omaha cuisine and will forevermore.

Chapter 2

OF TACOS AND THAI FOOD

Omaha's Diverse Past and Present

I was sitting at a Thai restaurant in downtown Omaha, pondering the meaning of life over a stellar, spicy plate of pad see ew. My thoughts quickly turned to food—nothing new there—and soon I was pondering, for the tenth time that week, what defines a good food scene. One thing that tends to come up over and over again is the concept of variety: what one wants, one shall receive. While it's true that Omaha might not (yet) offer you vegan Taiwanese fusion dumplings at 3:00 a.m. when that craving hits you once a year, there are countless eateries specializing in a particular type of cuisine—and killing it while they're at it.

It was 1:00 p.m. as I gobbled the last soy sauce–soaked broccoli floret from my plate, and every table in Bangkok Cuisine was occupied. This family-operated favorite—where the noodles come beautifully charred from the wok and the flavors are always impeccably balanced—has been in business since 1999, and really, its story is one of many. The fact is that Omahans enjoy an ever-expanding roster of restaurants to choose from, many of them a result of the higher-than-average influx of foreign-born populations over the years. Since 1857, when the city was incorporated, there have been a lot of good reasons to come to Omaha, and the food and traditions brought by generations of immigrants over the years went into creating this wonderfully diversified food scene. Allow me to explain.

Omaha started out as a town with a lot of promise, and that was very much on purpose. Its proponents—those successful businessmen from east of the Mississippi—fought hard to make Omaha the most important city for hundreds of miles. When Nebraska formally graduated from a U.S. territory to a U.S. state in 1867, Omaha lost the capital to Lincoln, where it remains today. But that's okay. Things were still looking up. Five years earlier, the Pacific Railroad Act had designated Union Pacific the company that would forge westward with railroad construction and meet its Californian counterpart, the Central Pacific Railroad, in the middle, thus making it possible to travel from one side of the country to the other.[19] Any kid worth his weight in floppy discs knew that before this, the oft-traveled Oregon Trail was the best option if you wanted to get anywhere near the West Coast. Needless to say, the odds were much better traveling by rail than by covered wagon that you wouldn't pick up a killer case of dysentery, so this whole "joining of the nation" thing was kind of a big deal. Omaha was chosen as Union Pacific's headquarters, and people looking for work lined up, many of them originally from lands far and wide.[20]

Our poetic pal J.H. Noteware, state superintendent of immigration around this time, broke it down for us in his 1873 pamphlet about why newcomers to the United States should head for Nebraska:

> *Nebraska will not be wanting in towns and cities. Her great valleys— broad, straight, smooth and long—lie in the right direction and relation to secure an effective system of Railways which in turn will create centers of commerce. So that, in a few years, the towns and villages will be neither few nor small; but healthy, vigorous, populous towns, consuming or exporting the products of the land, and giving back to the producers the necessities and luxuries of other countries.*
>
> *The rich soil, mild climate, favorable locality, Free Homesteads, and cheap investments in Nebraska, are being accepted by the most enterprising men and women of all nations. She will have the paramount advantages, secured from the collection in one arena, of the muscular strength and skill of all peoples, which will make Nebraska a land of physical, intellectual, moral and political power. Here come at once the restless Yankee, the patient German, the fiery Frenchman, the persistent Briton, the enduring Scandinavian, to blend their several industries and economies on this field of enterprise.[21]*

If you glazed over that extended quotation, the Cliff's version is that because of its prime locale on the spankin'-new railways, Nebraska was sure to attract both the brainiest *and* the brawniest. He then extended an exclusive invite to the people of Europe, plus America's East Coasters, because you know they were probably already whining about how expensive Manhattan was.

Until the gradual shift to trucks began in the 1920s, it was the railroads that provided cattle transportation from the sprawling prairies into livestock centers much like the ones that made South Omaha's human population grow like a weed.[22] And as we learned in the first chapter, those yards were yet another valuable source of employment for immigrants. It didn't hurt that Omaha became known as the "Gate City," providing the portal to California and the West, an identifier that people found quite attractive.[23] In the year 1900, a quarter of Omaha's population was born outside the United States, and about half of citizens' parents were foreign-born as well. This was a much greater percentage than the national average; Omaha was indeed exceptionally diverse at the time.[24] This trend continued into the twentieth and twenty-first centuries.

It's a good thing that the term "melting pot" has always made me think of fondue. That provides a lovely segue out of this immigration history lesson and into the meat and potatoes (or tacos and tostadas, as it were) of this chapter.

A Neighborhood Like No Other

It was 9:30 p.m. on a Thursday evening in late summer, a time when the genius idea of tacos will likely lead you to South Twenty-fourth Street, where other geniuses have already packed the area with their vehicles. Live mariachi music filled the air from the street. Nearly all of the restaurants were chock full: Taqueria Tijuana was brimming, as was Taqueria El Rey. One of the larger restaurants, El Dorado, had an open table. This was a three-taco kind of night, we realized, as all conversation stopped with the arrival of the complimentary chips and salsa. Luckily, the tacos arrived swiftly, corn tortillas cradling the al pastor–style pork, finely chopped onions and a flowery bunch of fresh cilantro. We briefly commented on the beauty of the shaved meat's spiced, deep-red edges before dousing in house-made hot sauce. Consumed in two or three bites. Repeat.

Of course, we could have opted for one block off the beaten path over to Twenty-fifth and Q, to a standalone storefront bearing the name La Choza, a word meaning "hut," which seems totally appropriate for this charming locale. This is a real gem, known not only for its tacos but also

Morning along South Twenty-fourth Street. *Author's collection.*

for the huaraches and pupusas. The latter is a Salvadoran specialty, a type of cornmeal flour patty usually filled with beans and cheese. I get mine also with loroco, a green vine flower that adds a crunchy effect the way a scallion would. Chicharrón, in this case a seasoned ground pork, is another favorite filling. I spend most of my time there marveling over how they keep each of them straight, since they all look virtually the same on the outside, so you can't tell which is which until you dig in. Topped with the accompanying fermented cabbage slaw and red sauce, with two or three of these babies you're good to go. There are a number of other joints to grab good pupusas in town, but in my experience none is quite as satisfying as La Choza.

A few blocks down the road, the aroma of roasting meats and frying tortillas quickly turns into something sweeter. I honestly wouldn't recommend going anywhere near the corner of Twenty-fifth and P if you have a sweet tooth you're trying to tame, for the scent of baked goods can be overpowering in these parts. For sixteen hours a day, seven days a week, pastries of all shapes and sizes are being turned out of this humble-looking operation called the International Bakery. Patrons grab a tray and a set of tongs at the door, pile on whatever they'd like from the bakery's rows of colorful offerings and pay at the register, where the goods are carefully wrapped and bagged by the staff. On one recent morning, I snagged one of the best slices of pound cake I've ever had the pleasure of purposefully omitting from my well-intentioned calorie count for the day. I also bagged a batch of sprinkle-studded *galletas* for the office that never quite made it to the office. The bakery is also known for its magnificent custom cakes. Again, you have been warned to stay away if you are trying to lay off the sweet stuff. With the scent of baked goods this place gives off, you simply won't stand a chance.

Perhaps it's wise to head a few blocks north to L Street, where you can earn your dessert by first having a proper meal. Jacobo's Mexican Grocery is my go-to before attending any sort of social get-together, so that I can arrive with armfuls of freshly prepared salsas, refried beans, seasoned rice and braised pork (carnitas) that's so tender and full of flavor it's what most people hover over at the party until it's gone. If you show up and there's a huge line at the prepared foods counter where you order this stuff by the pint, have no fear, for it moves quickly. I like to take a tamale for the road, rescuing it from its husk and popping it into my mouth before even getting to the car. Jacobo's has been at this game since 1976, more than earning its place as neighborhood mainstay.

Often lined with taco trucks—since long before food trucks were cool—South Twenty-fourth is known for being a hub of good flavors. Patrons can also browse the city's largest collection of imported Mexican pottery without leaving the block and behold the vibrant murals on sides of buildings in between rummaging through one of the many thrift shops and clothing stores. There's nowhere else quite like it.

SOUTH TWENTY-FOURTH STREET: HALLOWED GROUND FOR RESTAURANTS AND RETAIL

If you were a rancher from rural Nebraska in, say, 1926, you would have taken a cargo train from your town into Omaha along with your cattle, where you'd sell them off at the stockyards for a pretty penny. You'd then make your way from the brand-new Livestock Exchange Building, pockets stuffed with currency, a few blocks east on N Street to the commercial district on Twenty-fourth. Today, you can no longer follow in Mr. Rancher Man's footsteps, as the direct route has long been interrupted with the erection of Highway 75. But the Livestock Exchange Building still looms over the area, a ten-story brick beauty that's in use today as a clinic on the first two floors and two elegant ballrooms on the top floor largely utilized for wedding receptions, with renovated apartment units sandwiched in between.

The iconic Livestock Exchange Building in South Omaha. *Author's collection.*

It's possible that Mr. Rancher Man might have dined at nearby Johnny's Café, although it was still a little rough around the edges at that time. He most likely would have headed for Phillips Department Store, one of Omaha's largest behind J.L. Brandeis and Sons downtown. It was sort of like a Super Target, but with much better dining options. Today, a Rent-a-Center occupies the area where it once stood. Our rancher might have even caught a show at the brand-new Roseland Theatre. In the morning, he would have boarded a passenger train back home. Every return trip back to Omaha would have revealed a slightly bigger, better city. He would have interacted with a number of first-generation immigrants of Czech, German, Polish, Irish, Hungarian, Swedish, Danish and Mexican origin.[25] Today, you can still see surnames of the original building owners etched in stone above the doorways. The bricks sport remnants of painted signage, long washed away by the elements. South Omaha's city hall is in use today as a law office, and the post office, Omaha's oldest, is still a post office.

South Twenty-fourth Street is the subject of a walking tour led by the nonprofit Restoration Exchange Omaha, whose mission is to "educate and motivate the local community to restore and preserve older properties through education, advocacy and invigoration."[26] Vince Furlong, longtime advocate and tour leader, told me that the area started changing when increasing automobile ownership and a growing suburban contingency led to a fundamental shift in the city's urban landscape. It's a phenomenon not unique to Omaha at the time, and those around back then will certainly recall the mall boom of the 1960s. Constructed on large plots of empty land with ample parking stalls, places like Westroads, Southroads, Crossroads and the Center Mall became the new shopping experience of choice—a bad day for mom and pops but a great day for food courts.[27]

By the time the stockyards started to run out of steam, which coincided with the shift to mall shopping, it was game over for this commercial district. There was definitely a bit of a dark period in the '70s and '80s, when many of the storefronts sat vacant. The fire never totally flickered out, though, as there were still some jobs available in nearby meatpacking plants. Many families of European descent moved into other areas of town and took up jobs in other industries, some remaining in South Omaha and some opting for the lush greenery of West Omaha. The immigration numbers started shifting in favor of an incoming Latino population, and at the time, the Jacobo family was one of a few to provide the necessary amenities to the growing community.[28] In 1986, what would become the neighborhood's oldest sit-down Mexican restaurant, El Alamo, opened its doors.[29] By the '90s, the growth rate of the Latino population in Nebraska ranked tenth in the nation, and it continues to grow today.[30] The resulting boom of restaurants specializing in Mexican cuisine has been very fortunate for my twice-a-week taco cravings.

Other communities are represented in the food scene here, too. There's a massive Asian supermarket at Twenty-fifth and P and a very busy Thai place near Twenty-fourth and K called Laos Thai Restaurant. There are also some old standards on Twenty-fourth. One is Joe Tess Place, originally opened by Czech-born Joseph Tesnohlidek around 1940, where they're still serving tons of famous breaded and fried carp to a hyper-loyal clientele.[31] And at O Street, Eddie Galas from Poland opened Eddie's sandwich shop in 1951, a family-run business that's morphed over the years into a highly successful catering company. It's known for its stick-to-your-ribs kraut and dumplings.[32]

But still, if Mr. Western Nebraska Rancher from 1926 stepped into a time machine set for today, he would definitely be a little freaked at first by all of the changes, until he realized that most of the buildings he recognized were still intact. (I don't know about you, but I see a Hollywood film script somewhere in there.) One of the reasons South Twenty-fourth Street is unique is the continued use of original construction, somewhat of an anomaly in this neck of the woods. For all of the ways in which the area has changed over the past one hundred years, it still remains one of the busiest neighborhoods in town in terms of foot traffic. The annual Cinco de Mayo weekend, characterized by a large-scale throw-down of a parade, attracts thousands of spectators from all corners of Omaha. On many nights of the week, it can be tough to find an empty table in any one of the taquerias lining the street. And word to the wise: you'd better get to Jacobo's early before it runs out of beans.

THAT SHEELYTOWN FLAVOR

In nineteenth-century Omaha, your commute to work most likely resembled a short jaunt a few blocks outside your front door. Not to state the obvious, but it was important to live close to your place to employment in those days. And so goes the story of Sheely Bros. Packing Company, a plant just southeast of what is Hanscom Park today. At first, Irish populations settled here, followed by Czech and Polish, to work in the plant. It was one of the first plants, just as the industry was really taking off, and it had quickly grown to be the largest by 1884. I wouldn't want to be the unlucky soul responsible for the massive fire that burned the plant to the ground just two years later, never to be rebuilt.[33]

Located directly north of all the other action happening in the South Omaha Stockyards, the neighborhood known as Sheelytown continued to fill in with more immigrant workers tending to the industry in the 1880s. At one point, 95 percent of residents did not speak English. As with many solid immigrant areas of the period, Sheelytown earned a reputation for being rather rough-and-tumble. This was the old country, the bluest of collars, filled with dubious politicians, house fires and fistfights—or so the legend goes.[34] Heck, I wasn't there.

By the time Polish-born Frank Synowiecki opened Dinker's Bar in 1965, construction of both I-80 and I-480 had already sliced straight through Sheelytown. That didn't stop him from opening the place, but he did have to deal with a lovely six-lane highway virtually in the front yard of the restaurant. It has sat on that block ever since, a hub of fun for locals and the subject of numerous national write-ups over the years. Since adding a food menu, the number of times it has made "best burger" lists would send any newcomer to the scene quivering in his boots. Patrons order at the cash-only counter, take a number to their table and belly up separately to the bar should they want to imbibe. Sandwiches are served with a steak knife piercing each bun vertically, in baskets lined with red-and-white checkered paper. Patrons spill out onto the otherwise residential street with stomachs full and a slight buzz on. I imagine this is exactly the type of place the rest of the country thinks of when they think of Omaha cuisine. In answer to that, it's more accurately what Omahans think of when they think of Sheelytown cuisine.

YE OLE VINTON STREET

A mere one mile away from Dinker's, at Louie M's Burger Lust Café, owner Lou Marcuzzo splits his time between greeting guests and helping in the kitchen, as well as tending to other typical restaurant ownership duties, as he has since opening the place in 1980. He could probably do this type of thing with his eyes closed, having grown up in a restaurant family—his grandmother owned the Italian Gardens in the Little Italy neighborhood. Lou, a collector of restaurant memorabilia and knower of Omaha history factoids, told me about the way the neighborhood used to be.

His restaurant is located within the Vinton Street Commercial Historic District. The curvature of the road and quaint diagonal placement of the buildings makes you wonder: what's so special about this particular street? The answer likely has something to do with the fact that this was once a streetcar hub. The area is a bit too far away from the stockyards to get there on foot, even by old-timey standards, but once the Omaha Motor Railway erected a line that ran north–south on Twenty-fourth from N Street to Vinton, workers were free to move a little farther away than the backyard of the stockyards. They added a line that traveled all the way north to downtown Omaha, and the two converged on Vinton Street, making this a highly traveled thoroughfare in its day.[35]

From 1880 to 1940, there were more German immigrants in Omaha than any other single nationality.[36] Lou told me that Vinton Street began primarily German as well. He singled out the leadership of one man, an entrepreneur from the fatherland named Fritz Mueller. Herr Mueller arrived in Omaha in 1881 at age twenty-six and promptly got involved in everything he could, from local politics to hotel management. Lou told this story from across the booth as I sipped a cup of diner-rific coffee. "At one time, Fritz Mueller was the largest food purveyor in the U.S.," he declared. Indeed, things really picked up for Mueller when the Trans-Mississippi Exposition was held in Omaha in 1898. There, he invested in a Schlitz-branded beer pavilion that sat one thousand people at a time for weeks on end. After that, he made sure he did the same at other expositions nationwide.[37]

Mueller and a few other German entrepreneurs are responsible for building most of Vinton Street's seventeen structures that sit on the National Register of Historic Places. As is the case on South Twenty-fourth Street, most of these old buildings are still in use today, perpetuating the charming aesthetic the builders were surely aiming for. There are thrift stores, antique shops, butchers, art galleries and bars, most with erratic opening hours that keep the street feeling a little bit sleepier than you might expect. But Louie M's keeps things rolling along around here. With its cozy patio and ultra-colorful, cartoon-esque mural of burgers, fries and onion rings, it's the beacon of business that keeps people coming back.

Lou explained that his restaurant started when there was a dearth of breakfast establishments to serve the nearby businesses. Wanting to return to the food industry after a stint in corporate America, he bought the building from Fritz Mueller's sons. At first, it was meant to be a catering business. But soon the neighbors asked him to put a pot of coffee on. He speaks gently, a real storyteller. He told me that the restaurant's goofy name was for no reason other than to appease a friend's goofy suggestion, and the myriad hot sauces on each table can simply be attributed to the fact that he likes hot sauce—nothing more. The walls are plastered with posters of 1950s celebrities and old family photos, along with various maps and menus. Stuff Lou likes, basically. I do appreciate the sentiment of not taking oneself too seriously.

A famous Louie M's burger will get you a toasty bun, melty cheese and a hand-formed patty. Breakfast is served all day. Most of the clientele are regulars. And yet there's no Schlitz on the menu—I do wonder what Herr Mueller would think of that if he were around today.

Omaha still has a strong reverence for German culture. You'd be hard-pressed to not run into some sort of Oktoberfest event every fall, for example. But things were just never the same after World War I kicked up in 1914, especially once the United States went into battle in 1917. Up until then, there had been a very active German-American Alliance of Nebraska that provided a unified voice for the population and acted somewhat as an agent for cultural preservation. It became dramatically uncool to show emotional attachment for Germany during the war, though, and the alliance ultimately fizzled out.[38]

There have been a handful of German restaurants throughout the years, but very few remain. One, owned by Gerda Bailey, originally of Augsburg, Germany, sits at the corner of Fifty-second and Leavenworth Streets, with the words "German Bäckerei Restaurant" painted several feet tall on the side of the building. (No need for subtlety here.) The menu is limited to just a few entrées; it's truly as if Mrs. Bailey is your German grandmother cooking for you, in particular the goulash and jägerschnitzel. The pastries and breads are made from recipes that you can imagine are executed entirely from memory, and if you associate Germans in Omaha with nothing else, it should be this amazing *Apfelstrudel.*

"DUMPLINGS AND KRAUT TODAY AT THE BOHEMIAN CAFÉ"

With its wide sidewalks shaded by tall trees, South Thirteenth Street's aesthetic is one of my favorites in the city. Clearly, Omaha's Czech population thought the same when they started arriving in droves in the 1880s. These days, you kind of have to look for signs of a once-stealthy Czech presence here—there's the Prague Hotel and the Sokol Auditorium but not much else. One attraction you cannot miss, without a doubt the most well known and loved, is the Bohemian Café.

The restaurant first opened at another location a half block up the road in 1924, coincidentally the same year the Immigration Reform Act made it more difficult for newcomers to move to the United States. Then, in 1959, it relocated to its present location at 1256 South Thirteenth. From an architectural standpoint, they just don't make restaurants like this anymore. A large, sturdy awning supported by thick pillars marks the exterior, along with floral decorated tiles and windows of brightly colored stained glass

Front of the Bohemian Café, postcard. *Courtesy of Douglas County Historical Society.*

Bohemian Café's Svickova entrée. *Author's collection.*

throughout. A neon sign across the street, having also become a well-known Thirteenth Street fixture, directs patrons to the reserved parking lot. Like at Cascio's, it's the norm to see older couples escort each other arm in arm to their early dinners, and like at Cascio's, this sight has the power of restoring my faith in marriage—at least for a few minutes. If you're on foot passing by in the morning, you will catch the scent of rich, warming chicken broth that will make you want to drop whatever you're doing and go on inside to enjoy a cup. Or maybe you'll opt for the specialty: the liver dumpling soup.

During one visit, I overheard a woman in a thick German accent bemoaning the lack of boiled beef—they only offer it on certain days of the week. I thought to myself that perhaps she should choose something else off of the sizable menu. But a big part of what the Bohemian does is just that: cater to old-timers who want their traditional meals. Similar to Johnny's and other restaurants born of this era, the recipes are as straightforward as they are pleasing. The svickova, a marinated, braised beef with a creamy gravy, would be the entrée to try first. Nearly every main comes flanked by two ginormous bread dumplings—a mixture of flour, milk, eggs and bread cubes that absorb the gravy beautifully—and your choice of two types of kraut.

The portions are hilariously large. My suggestion is to be pragmatic about how you handle it: the sooner you get a to-go box, the more space you will have for dessert—and another beer. Co-owner Marsha Bogatz attributed the large portions to their desire to please. "If you leave here hungry, we are doing something wrong," she said. The featured dessert, on the other hand, a wonderful fruit-filled pastry called *kolacky*, is a manageable size.

Marsha and her brother, Terry Kapoun, both third-generation owners, have been manning the restaurant for years. The place is a real fixture in the community, with constant bookings for family functions by the people who've kept them in business as one of Omaha's oldest restaurants. Let's not pretend, though, that the Bohemian Café regularly attracts a young, sprightly crowd—it doesn't. But it's one of the few places where you can give your imagination a rest if you want to transport to the eastern European countryside from a time long gone—in this environment, you're basically already there. It's a portal to the past, one that shouldn't go unappreciated. Who knows—it could eventually go the way that so many classics have in recent years.

Speaking of the past, should you want to relive the Bohemian Café radio jingle that populated the airwaves and perpetually got stuck in listeners' heads for many years, the lyrics go like this:

> *Dumplings and kraut today*
> *At Bohemian Café*
> *Draft beer that's sparkling, plenty of parking*
> *See you at lunch, Okay?*

Yes, Omaha Has a Little Italy

Standing at the northwest corner of Seventh and Pacific Streets on a recent gusty spring afternoon, I was bothered by the wind only in the way that it kept whipping street dust and wayward pieces of my own hair into my eyes as I pat around my bag for my prescription glasses. Besides the unsavory bits of dirt that blew into my mouth, I was cool with the uncooperative midwestern spring weather. The wind, in fact, was ushering over an enticing aroma from the place across the street that I really can't get enough of. My eyes shot from a lifetime glued to computer screens, I finally located my glasses and deciphered the sign. "Est. 1919," it read, framed by red, white and green paint representing the Italian flag. I had thought that's what it said but couldn't really believe my eyes because that's mighty old. The eatery before me was Orsi's Bakery, a neighborhood staple in Little Italy, Omaha.

Every single morning of the year, besides a handful of holidays, owner Jim Hall is there at an ungodly hour, mixing dough and forming loaves of Italian-style white bread. Orsi's supplies fresh bread to a bunch of local establishments, including Gorat's and the Bohemian Café, so there's always a tall order to fill. In the span of time it took to ask him a few simple questions about what his day is like, he had formed three or four perfect loaves ready to go into the oven, seemingly on autopilot. He's the face of the place, the guy you are most likely to talk to if you come into the shop. He and his wife, Kathy, purchased Orsi's directly from the Orsi family in 2010, so there hasn't been any lapse in quality or integrity in nearly one hundred years of business.[39]

Had it not been for a fire in the '90s, it would have been in this same building that the original Orsi brothers started mimicking their Italian counterparts back home, taking dough and spreading it evenly in a pan, topping it with all-day red sauce and a bit of cheese and offering room-temperature squares of it as an anytime snack to patrons who would come in for their bread orders. The most common description I hear about Orsi's is something to the effect of, "It's not really like pizza…it's more like really good bread with toppings on it." As it turns out, that is quite the point. Orsi's

The all-important baking tools at Orsi's Bakery. *Author's collection.*

makes pizza the old-fashioned, Italian bakery way, and people have been digging that for a really, really long time.

The phone rings periodically throughout the morning with preorders, but around 11:00 a.m. is when the operation really picks up. It starts to feel a bit like controlled chaos. Jim and one or two other employees handle it all, preparing the large sheets of pizza to order, placing them in the huge rotating oven and letting them stand for just a minute before packaging them up. Jim slows down his hurried demeanor when he talks to you out at the register; he could have ten things going in the back, but you never really feel like you're bugging him.

The pizza comes in full-, half- or quarter-sheet size, and they also do an individual-sized mini. The Orsi's full sheet makes regular appearances at company lunches and family get-togethers. It's really the way to go. I've said before that I am "Orsi'd out," but that doesn't stop me from reaching into the box a few minutes later. Orsi's also features freshly baked ricotta cookies, imported pastas and other Italian specialties. From the deli, patrons order sliced meats like soppressata, mortadella and prosciutto di Parma, as well as cheeses like Parmigiano-Reggiano. Grab a loaf of bread and you've got yourself a picnic. There is no seating room; this is strictly a takeout biz.

As I left with my giant box of hot pizza nearly as wide as the door frame, Jim asked where I've parked. I tried to protest and say that I've got it, but he authoritatively reminded me that he's done this before. "People say they've got it, and then they wind up with cheese and sauce dumped all over the inside of their car and onto the street and then they come in wanting another pizza." I smiled at the passionate insistence. He's so right!

Orsi's is one of the only eateries left of what was once a vibrant, excessively popular dining hub. Little Italy, the neighborhood stretching from South Tenth Street to the Missouri River and Pacific to Center Streets, used to be the place to go on Friday nights for its high concentration of trendy restaurants—so much that one of Lou Marcuzzo's fondest memories from growing up around there is the legendary traffic jams caused by Omahans coming in from all corners of town. Ask anyone around at the time, and they'll give you the roll call of beloved restaurants that were popular in the '50s and '60s and mostly shut down by the end of the '70s.

One by the name of Caniglia's started off similar to Orsi's as a bakery around the same time. After World War II, it evolved into one of Omaha's first pizzerias and, later, into the Original Caniglia's Steakhouse. The children and grandchildren of owners Cirino and Giovanna, natives of Sicily, went on to open a litany of other Italian-themed restaurants bearing

The glitz and glamour of Mr. C's Steakhouse. *Courtesy of Douglas County Historical Society.*

the Caniglia name. Today, they're revered as one of Omaha's first great restaurant families, although the final survivor, Caniglia's Venice Inn, closed in 2014.[40] Another, Mr. C's Steak House, is still remembered today for its gaudiness for the sake of being gaudy. A friend once told me that it was like Christmas year-round, that it was the only restaurant to elude boredom as a child, since there was so much to look at.

Yes, the Caniglias definitely knew what the people liked. The family ties around here ran deep; even Joe Piccolo's wife, Grace, was Cirino and Giovanna's daughter. Aside from the endearing midwestern tendency to pronounce Italian as "Eye-talian," this is a pretty authentic neck of the woods. There's still a playful territorialism present: "Parking for Italians Only," reads one driveway sign, and another implores passersby to kindly collect their dog's sh*t, in Italian. A few groups of brightly colored stucco buildings draw on inspiration from Europe's best peninsula, and a ridiculously hilly terrain can make you feel like you're climbing through the Alps. Many of the older residences have been razed and replaced, and a series of white townhomes characterizes the two-story skyline on what has come to be known as "Caniglia Plaza." All that remains of the first Caniglia eatery is one rather conspicuous piece of public art where the restaurant once stood: a thirteen-foot-tall stainless steel rendition of a fork taming a pile of spaghetti. It's a fantastic photo op for fans of oversized depictions of everyday food items, but it leaves something to be desired in this once-bustling part of town.

We've got Cascio's still going strong up on Tenth Street. And the Sons of Italy still hosts spaghetti dinners, as it has been doing for a million years. Still, one young buck of a college student I spoke to recently didn't even realize that Omaha had a Little Italy section at all. If that seems like kind of a shame, you'll be pleased to know that developers have been hovering over the area, eager to transform it into the next big thing. And just like that, Little Italy is on the cusp of making a return to young Omahans' vernacular in a big way.

The Comfort of Home

Food has the ability to travel with people—it's not hard to connect those dots. That's a big part of why again and again we see highly diverse cuisines across the country, and especially in Omaha. This principle was echoed by culinary historian Adrian Miller in his 2013 book *Soul Food: The Surprising Story of an American Cuisine, One Plate at a Time.* The tendency of food to travel with its families and fans must have been on Miller's mind when he considered the inherent difference between two important types of cuisine. "I think of soul food as the limited repertoire of Southern food," he told NPR in an interview. "And it's really about the food that black migrants from the South took with them to other parts of the country. And they did what other migrants do when they got to a new place—they tried to re-create home often through food."[41]

We see this idea of extending home through food over and over again. On the soul food tip, we see it with Patricia Barron (aka Big Mama) of Big Mama's Kitchen. She loves to serve items she grew up eating. The cold fried chicken sandwich on the menu at Big Mama's Sandwich Shop, for example, is a version of the one she and her family would prepare in bulk to eat on road trips.[42] Restaurants in North Omaha like Big Mama's and Lonnelle's Southern Delight, another excellent soul food locale, embody that idea of "home" perfectly. For me it's impossible to not equate home with comfort, and here that's the whole experience—the animal print tablecloths at Big Mama's and the huge portions of collard greens and mac and cheese at Lonnelle's. Favorite standards like Jim's Rib Haven and Time Out Chicken elevate North Omaha's comfort food scene to the point of near-perfection. Both are the best at what they do.

Comfort can also be found in a steaming bowl of pho at Chef Be Lam's Saigon Surface downtown, where the rice noodles enveloped in a rich, complex beef broth can keep you occupied for the better part of an hour. Omaha's lucky in that diners can take their pick of fabulous pho places—there's Omelet & Viet Cuisine, Pho Viet and the original Saigon, among others. Thai cuisine's answer to the traditionally Vietnamese pho is found in the exquisite beef noodle soup at the notoriously busy Salween Thai. Ethiopian dining is represented in places like the popular Lalibela and Ethiopian Restaurant, each offering traditional injera bread entrées with wonderfully spiced beans, meats and veggies. And there really is nothing quite like a plate of fried plantains at Caribbean Delight on North Seventy-second Street, at least in terms of comfort food.

The famous Jim's in North Omaha. *Author's collection.*

Two-piece meal from Time Out Chicken. *Author's collection.*

Oftentimes, the desire to make it a homey experience really shines through for the customer. That would be the case with John's Grecian Delight, where John Sakkas has been slicing gyro meat for his regular patrons since 1981 in the lower level of the Southroads Mall, now Southroads Technology Park. His mantra involves taking care of your customers, and they will take care of you.[43] Other Greek restaurants that have also been around forever, places like Greek Islands and Jim and Jennie's Greek Village, would say the same.

And of course, some of the ultimate comfort food can be found in dim sum cuisine. The basic premise of dim sum involves planting oneself in a chair on a weekend, sipping tea gathered around family and friends and sharing as many small plates as one can possibly muster. Fortunately, Omaha has no shortage of of dim sum places. And if you're not predisposed to sharing, well, the siu mai pork dumplings at Grand Fortune are worth fighting over.

Omaha's food scene today is difficult to delineate into neat little boxes of "they came here during this time and they brought this food with them." The important part is that we enjoy the assortment we've got. When chef Rene Orduña opened Dixie Quicks in downtown Omaha in the mid-'90s, for example, there weren't any other places around serving Cajun, southern and southwestern cuisine. "We

RENE ORDUÑA/DIXIE QUICKS
······ TOMATO BUTTER ······

✓ **Unsalted butter**   ✓ **Whole peeled plum tomatoes, canned**
✓ **Garlic, parsley, salt, and pepper to taste**

1) Combine equal parts butter and tomatoes.

2) Add as much garlic, parsley, salt, and pepper as you may want.

3) Place ingredients in microwave briefly until butter is just about melted.

4) Use an immersion blender to grind it all up.

5) Serve with seafood, steaks, eggs, anything!

6) Can be kept in the fridge for up to a week.

were it," he told me. Today, the Cajun influence is mellow, felt in the way the rich tomato butter drizzles off of the crab cakes, for example. It's at this point you realize that re-creating home through food doesn't need to be taken so literally— it's more a state of mind. If that's what Rene's going for here, along with all of the other wonderfully diverse restaurants in Omaha, he's got that down.

Chapter 3

PIZZA

A Case Study

I was sitting with a seven-year-old at a busy pizza place in Midtown Manhattan, both of us silent except for the faint sounds of chewing. The lad, who had mostly grown up in Omaha, had heard great things about New York and its pizza from various family members who've called the city home at one point or another. We had told him that New Yorkers walk and eat pizza at the same time—that it's just a way of life. The kid really took this to heart. Back in Omaha, he'd even taken to practicing his pizza eating in preparation. (So the next time you see a little guy doing laps around the perimeter of the pizza place, proudly showing off his fold technique while intently concentrating on not biting his tongue in the midst of this advanced exercise in multitasking, that's probably what's going on.)

Upon arrival, the second order of business after climbing the Empire State was a piping-hot slice o' pie, and so there we sat, in the shadows of behemoth buildings and more tourists than Disneyland in France. Keeping it real and sticking to pepperoni.

It's ubiquitous. It's inexpensive. The New York slice *is* actually a way of life. The thing is, it's also inconsistent. I just want to go ahead and burst that bubble, bust the myth that New York pizza is unquestionably the best. The problem with this particular slice was the grainy quality of the crust. Perhaps the dough guy was having a bad day, or it was reheated too long. The point is that bad pizza can happen in New York, too. It can happen anywhere. It happens in Omaha from time to time. But that doesn't necessarily stop lines

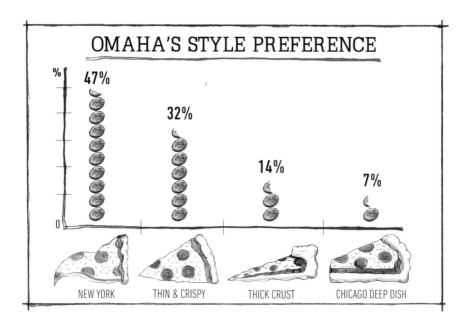

of hungry people from forming, shuffling up to the counter one by one eager to take in these precious calories.

There are lots of opinions out there about the secret to a good pie, as well as where Omaha fits into that enigma. According to a 2015 survey, a whopping 93 percent of respondents claim that pizza is one of their favorite foods.[44] And yet, only 26 percent of Omahans believe that the city has its own distinct style. And then there's the gigantor pizza chain founded and headquartered in Omaha by the name of Godfather's. Despite more than five hundred stores in thirty-six states opening since its founding in '73, more than one-third of us have indicated that we are not too keen on this national pizza maker rooted here.

So do we wish we were something else? About 47 percent say that their preferred style is the New York–inspired, floppy, foldable, lovable, cheesy, saucy slice. It made me wonder if any adults out there have ever practiced their "walk and eat" in preparation for a trip out east, too. And it made me want to dig deeper into Omaha's pizza-eating population. What's the deal with pizza here? Where do you get the stuff everyone loves?

What We Talk About When We Talk About Pizza

To declare oneself the "All-Knowing Supreme Pizza Eater of the Universe" would be like saying you speak every language in the world. I believe we are all pizza experts to some degree. (Except for fans of those single-serve microwavable Lean Cuisine pizzas. They are not pizza experts.) Allow me to break down for you the terms in which Omaha pizza will be discussed.

Crust

They say it's the New York water that makes the pizza crust there unique. Perhaps. It's probably more like good water in general leads to good dough. I think the most important quality to consider with crust is whether it can hold up under whatever's been baked on top of it. Ever do a one-handed slice grab only to have the crust pathetically droop and leave most of the cheese and toppings still in the box, casualties of careless baking skills and the laws of gravity? Second to a soggy crust and the dampened mood it brings is the flavor. With the majority of a pizza's flavor coming from what's on top, it's easy to forget that crust has potential to blow you away, too. That is, until you experience an extra-tasty one. More than 75 percent of Omahans surveyed indicated that crust is the best part of the pizza. That means three out of every four of us are the type who would motion to their significant other's crust graveyard while out on a date and ask, "Are you going to eat that?" Crust must jolly well be important to us, then. Surely it must be.

Cheese, Sauce and Other Toppings

Omahans, in general, like their toppings. I get the sense that a plain cheese slice would seem utterly naked to most of us, like an artist's poor, half-finished final work. We like our toppings so well that we frequently place them under the cheese, even on a pizza that's otherwise "New York style," a practice rooted in sacrilege according to some circles. The reason for this, I am told, is to accommodate more toppings, with the cheese acting as the protective canopy holding everything together. Sauces tend to vary widely across Omaha, from bright, summery raw crushed tomatoes to a deep-red, seasoned paste. And we are not usually at want for more cheese—it's typically layered on there pretty thick.

Tradition

Forget Democrat and Republican. The real conflict in Omaha exists when there's a disagreement on where to order pizza. We are extremely loyal to our favorites. We love La Casa's pastry-like edges so much that we'd pay $100 to have them delivered across the country by air—should we ever have the gall to move out of town. We keep Mama's Pizzeria on Saddle Creek Road bursting a little uncomfortably at its seams, filling its parking lot on any given school night mostly with giant SUVs full of families. An outsider might be surprised by the presence of a very strong pizza tradition in Omaha, but it's there in full force. And we are willing to fight for it.

At the same time, we embrace the new. About 66 percent of us claim that when a new pizza place opens in town, we are motivated to try it right away. We like being the first to the Yelp board (or the water cooler) with the opinion of the new place. Someone asks you how it was, and you clear your throat, center the spotlight and jump up on the soapbox. If Omahans ate pizza four times per month (and 30 percent say that they do), it would be thrice from an old favorite and once from a new kid on the block. It's a balance of traditional and new, always.

THE OMAHA WAY

26% AGREE — OMAHA HAS ITS OWN DISTINCT PIZZA STYLE

66% AGREE — BRAND NEW PIZZA PLACES ARE WORTH A TRY RIGHT AWAY

83% AGREE — PIZZA IN OMAHA IS BETTER TODAY THAN IT USED TO BE

BIGGER THAN BEEF

THE BIRTH OF PIZZA IN OMAHA

It's the early '50s again here in the world of this book—1953, to be exact. The doors had just opened at Omaha's newest restaurant, located in a converted home on Leavenworth Street. It was one of the first sit-down restaurants in town devoted to pizza, and most likely because of this fact, the place was hopping. Proud owner Joe Patane had an inkling that there were more than a few war veterans in town who had gotten to know the joys of the saucy stuff from their time abroad, specifically those who had been deployed around Naples. Up until now, Omahans could pretty much only get their pizza on by visiting Caniglia's down in Little Italy, and even that hadn't been around very long. We ached for a proper pizza. Patane saw a need, a want, a longing, for Omahans to revel in all of the cheese-filled, Euro-inspired glory. This was the same year that Dean Martin's ode to Italian-style love filled the airwaves. "When the moon hits your eye like a big pizza pie," the song goes. "That's amore."

Although pizza originated in Italy, most Italians outside Naples didn't really know what it was until after the war ended, which was roughly the same time Americans were discovering it, too.[45] That was why Joe Patane, who had moved to Omaha from Catania, Sicily, in 1914 at the age of eighteen, became enlightened through pizza pretty much along with everyone else. A trip to New York City was really what started it all. There was already a bit of a food movement going on there, with pizza becoming more and more popular and well known as an Italian invention due largely, again, to the returning military forces identifying it as such. Patane, who was a carpenter by trade, saw this opportunity and decided to cut his teeth as a restaurateur. So the fifty-seven-year-old got to work, perfecting his pizza recipe and fashioning a restaurant in what was once a house. He would call the place La Casa, a nod to that very fact.

This story was unfolding for me right at the original restaurant, told by two of Patane's grandchildren, Nicole Jesse and Joel Hahn, both co-owners and managers of the restaurant today. They told me that their grandfather's rich, pastry-like dough and rectangular sheet pan preparation was all very much on purpose. He didn't want to replicate exactly what he had seen in New York; rather, he strove to create something entirely new. At the same time, he wanted to leverage the popularity of beef in the area. "He figured, 'If I can incorporate beef into the pizza, then I've got my drawing card,'" Joel told me. This was all done according to the pre-locavore tenet of Italian cooking that states to use what's available to you. Add a little onion and a little seasoning and thus the Classic Hamburger pizza topping was born. Patane adjusted the recipe specifically so that the dough and hamburger would work in harmony. The exact ingredients, of course, are for them to know and for us to enjoy.

The words "made with 100% prime ground beef" indeed struck a chord with early pizza enthusiasts. Not only did La Casa run out of food halfway through its first evening in business, but it has also gone on to be one of Omaha's longest-running restaurants, and it shows no signs of stopping. That's not to say there weren't tough times. Nicole and Joel revealed that in the '70s the rise of chain restaurants nearly drove La Casa's business into a dead end. That, and the general shift of the city's population from east to west around the same time. But they credit their regulars with keeping the restaurant alive during this time, and with the public's shift back toward favoring locally owned restaurants, things are running smoothly these days. Many even consider the La Casa Classic Hamburger to be the epitome of the Omaha pizza style. Nicole and Joel might argue that since there's really no one else doing quite what they're doing, it doesn't really qualify as a style all on its own.

And still, others credit the Caniglia family with introducing pizza to the city. Nuncio "Eli" Caniglia was one of Giovanna and Cirino's sons, the couple who owned the bakery down near Orsi's in Little Italy. Eli was one of those GIs who had returned home from the war with a newfound taste for pizza, convincing his parents to put it on their menu. Eventually, in 1957, he opened his own pizzeria called Caniglia's Venice Inn. It was popular up until it closed in 2014, when Eli's sons, Chuck and Jerry, had surpassed the age of retirement.[46]

It's hard to imagine a time before pizza, but even more frightening is realizing that it wasn't that long ago. Regardless of which restaurateur actually "brought" pizza to Omaha, it surely would have happened anyway, as it was happening all over the country. La Casa's pie in particular has bred its own brand of fandom, Nicole told me. "A few years ago, there was a gentleman, a regular, who was picking up his pizza to go. He turns to me and says, 'I don't care what you charge me or what you do, but you've got a social responsibility to keep this restaurant open.'"[47]

ALWAYS WANTED TO BE ITALIAN

With pizza firmly implanted in the hearts and minds of Omahans everywhere, enter one young, aspiring restaurant owner by the name of Robert Tim Peffer. Most people call him Tim. He learned the inner workings of the industry in the institutional kitchens at Iowa State University before moving on to managing a Minsky's Pizza in Council Bluffs in 1978. The story goes that with a line out the door one Friday night, he turned to his brother, Walt, and said, "We could be doing this for ourselves, you know." At the urging of Walt's Italian wife, who claimed that Walt had "always wanted to be Italian, too," the two brothers of German and Irish descent opened a place on North Thirtieth Street in Florence with an appropriate Italophile name: Pefferoni's.

But as it was thirty-seven years later when I was told this, all of the Pefferoni's are now long gone. Still, it's an incredible story, of a restaurant ballooning to sixteen locations in three states in a matter of a few years. Good pizza was at the heart of it, but the business wasn't devoid of gimmicks: one location on Fiftieth and Dodge housed its salad bar on top of a modified automobile that happened to be a sexy-as-hell 1955 Austin-Healey sports car, complete with lettuce on the hood and croutons at the rear. No matter what kind of shtick Tim and Walt Peffer were up to, they knew how to get people in the door, and for seven years they rode the wave of pizza fever that was sweeping the nation along with the likes of Godfather's, Pizza Hut and other chains.

In 1987, Tim broke off from Walt to start his own restaurant, and Pefferoni's eventually became a thing of the past. Since then, Tim has been overseeing his longest-standing restaurant to date, Sgt. Peffer's Cafe Italian. A born storyteller, he spends a good chunk of time every day conversing with customers, many of whom have donated Beatles-themed memorabilia throughout the years. "These were all brought in by regulars," Tim said, motioning toward the walls and walls of Beatles swag. Thanks to that, the restaurant has successfully paired the checkered tablecloth Italian American eatery look with that of a mega-shrine to the Fab Four. It works, somehow. Now one of three Sgt. Peffer's locations, this sunny little restaurant on North Saddle Creek Road is a favorite to many: orders of five-cheese white pizza, tortellini with alfredo sauce and bowls of soup with seriously delicious homemade rolls fly out of the kitchen at a rapid rate. This is where Tim Peffer laid out for me his take on what Omaha-style pizza is. I figured I'd better listen to the guy who's been in the Omaha pizza business for four decades.

What Omaha Pizza May Be

Tim contended that the kind of pizza preferred most by the Omaha contingent starts with a thicker crust that's got a slight chewiness to it. While we're not talking Chicago deep dish thick, there's definitely a density here necessitated by all of the other stuff that gets piled on top. The seasoned tomato sauce should be fresh, but otherwise it plays second fiddle in this production; in Tim's words, it's "enough sauce on there just to know you've got sauce on there." The cheese, on the other hand, is extremely important, both in quantity and quality. It's got to be a combination of part skim mozzarella, to brown up nicely, and whole mozzarella, to stay nice and stretchy—and there should be plenty of it.

And then come the toppings. "If you're in Omaha, you've got to have lots of toppings," he explained with a certain frankness. There are plenty to choose from, but as we know, the one that stands out is hamburger, sometimes referred to simply as "beef topping." Having worked in pizzerias in central Iowa, where sausage tends to be the favorite, Tim can attest that the popularity of hamburger topping rises dramatically once you cross the state line into Nebraska. At Sgt. Peffer's, the seasoned, cooked beef goes underneath the cheese rather than on top in order to effectively hold all of the goodness inside. For the record, Tim

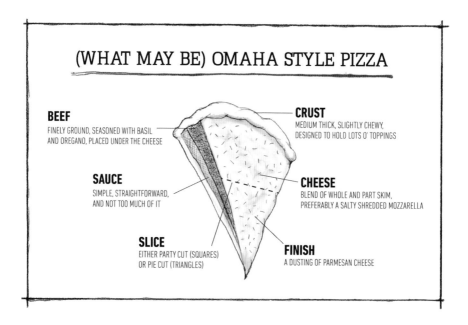

(WHAT MAY BE) OMAHA STYLE PIZZA

BEEF
FINELY GROUND, SEASONED WITH BASIL AND OREGANO, PLACED UNDER THE CHEESE

CRUST
MEDIUM THICK, SLIGHTLY CHEWY, DESIGNED TO HOLD LOTS O' TOPPINGS

SAUCE
SIMPLE, STRAIGHTFORWARD, AND NOT TOO MUCH OF IT

CHEESE
BLEND OF WHOLE AND PART SKIM, PREFERABLY A SALTY SHREDDED MOZZARELLA

SLICE
EITHER PARTY CUT (SQUARES) OR PIE CUT (TRIANGLES)

FINISH
A DUSTING OF PARMESAN CHEESE

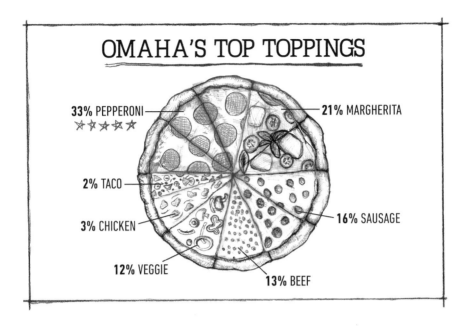

OMAHA'S TOP TOPPINGS

33% PEPPERONI

2% TACO

3% CHICKEN

12% VEGGIE

21% MARGHERITA

16% SAUSAGE

13% BEEF

prefers to cut his pie into triangles instead of squares, unless requested to do otherwise. But that decision is subject to the preference of the pizza maker.

Now, of course there are going to be limitations and disagreements on whether there's actually an Omaha pizza style. But look around: Mama's Pizza opened around the same time as Sgt. Peffer's, and its approach appears to be similar. And then there's Godfather's. The first location of the now-ubiquitous national pizza chain opened up near Eighty-fourth and Q Streets in 1973. When broken down ingredient by ingredient, its pizza is not unlike the Omaha pizza style in discussion.

About 44 percent of Omahans surveyed ranked hamburger topping within their top three choices. It didn't quite beat out pepperoni, our nation's undisputed darling, but it gave sausage a run for its money. Say what you will about our crust, sauce and cheese. No matter your exact preferences, we can all agree that hamburger topping is quintessential Omaha stuff. That it has the power to confound out-of-towners with its popularity is somewhat comical—and who doesn't like a good inside joke?

WHERE PIZZA REIGNS SUPREME

One crisp October eve back in 2009, hunger struck during hour eight of a multi-location Omaha dive bar excursion. The Valentino's Pizzeria on Leavenworth Street was there to answer the call. A standard pepperoni and mushroom, rectangular-shaped pie appeared in front of me at the takeout window in exchange for something like twenty dollars. But upon bringing the first slice up to my lips, I noticed that the pizza didn't look all that great. The same cannot be said of the Valentino's of years past. The Lincoln-bred pizza chain was founded in 1957 by a hardworking local couple before being sold in 1971. It subsequently expanded to a franchised chain of about forty stores. At some point, it was quite good—or at least, it was what people had to work with. Tim Peffer reminisced, "It used to be, if you wanted pizza, you'd drive down to Lincoln and go to Valentino's." It's even rumored that one of the creators of the original Godfather's recipe once went dumpster diving at a Valentino's to find out what kind of cheese it was using.[48] As pizza got more and more popular throughout the '70s and '80s, it would seem that quality became harder to control. I'm reminded of the touristy slice shop in Manhattan where the crust was weird and mealy. The cold, hard reality is that bad pizza exists. This eventual decline in quality that became so rudely apparent on that night I ordered Valentino's just might be a byproduct of success.

Of course, quality is all relative. And according to 82 percent of residents, pizza offerings in Omaha are of a higher quality today than they used to be. One thing is for sure: when nearly three hundred folks show up on a Tuesday night to sample fifteen different pizzas at a wall-to-wall, sold-out event, things are looking pretty bright. Such is the case at Omaha's Largest Pizza Review, an annual shindig put on by local digest *Food & Spirits Magazine*. Standing outside of the Waiting Room, the live music venue with the impeccable sound system where this has been going on for the past several years, people are clamoring to get in an hour before show time. When the thing finally kicks off, it's gleeful pandemonium, a madhouse of enjoyment. Local bands perform, but with attendees' hands full of food and drink, they do so to sparse applause. It's cool. They understand. By the end of it, there will be no crust unnibbled, no box unturned. Votes will be cast, and a new reigning champion, a new eaters' choice, will be announced. At the end, walking away from it all, you feel the kind of energized satisfaction usually reserved for when your favorite band strikes its last chord—except hopefully you're not quite as sweaty.

I talked to Erik Totten, the man responsible for both *Food & Spirits Magazine* and this huge pizza event. He was at once surprised and not so

Omaha's Largest Pizza Review, at the Waiting Room in Benson. *Author's collection.*

surprised at the success of the thing. "I tried to do this with barbecue, really good barbecue, and we had three hundred pounds of leftovers. But then when we do pizza, it sells out, and we run out of food every single year." (For the record, the food is typically donated, and event proceeds go to charity.) "Pizza engenders a response particularly here in Omaha that no other food item can replicate," said Erik, a native of small-town Nebraska who once called both North Carolina and California home. "I've thought about this a lot: is it just pizza anywhere, or is it pizza in Omaha?" Erik took a rare pause in order to contemplate this mystery. "I don't really get it."

The idea behind Omaha's Largest Pizza Review was originally to give smaller, family-owned pizzerias a platform to reach a new audience without having to spend a bunch of advertising money; it was much less about electing a winner. "The first one was just kind of an experiment—will people even come to this? And it was immediately apparent that, yes, people will definitely come to this," Erik reminisced. Students from the Institute for the Culinary Arts at Metropolitan Community College provide the focused, steady hands necessary to serve about one hundred slices per minute event-wide. "We basically tell them this is training for the biggest lunch rush you might ever have, and it's all over in about forty-five minutes." It's a beautiful sight, with non-traditional pies like savory pear and goat cheese sharing space on your paper plate with the classics. I almost sold my extra pair of tickets for double what I paid—yes, they were so in demand they were scalpable. But I chose to instead rub elbows with other diehard pizza devotees. It was worth it.

Topics Hotter than an Eight-Hundred-Degree Wood-Fire Oven

Boy, do we love pizza. About 90 percent of us eat it at least once a month, and 93 percent emphatically claim it as one of our favorite foods. Granted, there's a slight chance this respondent pool is a bit skewed since they voluntarily elected to fill out a survey on this very topic, but can we look past that? Do you know any pizza haters? If so, do you trust them? To say Omahans are more passionate about pizza than your average U.S. city would be conjecture; nevertheless, it sure does come up in casual conversation a lot.

Sometimes it feels like we agree on nothing. One respondent sounded off about Big Fred's, a local institution since 1965, claiming that it is "terrible and weird." Another expressed resounding enthusiasm: "Big Fred's has the best pizza!!" That's with two exclamation points, people. There is also a sizable schism present within hamburger topping ideology. I was told by one commenter, quite poignantly, that "hamburger on pizza is a sin." Another took it a step further, calling the concept "an affront to God herself." And still others consider it "our best option." Clearly, we are more divided on this than we think.

In general, we are really quite hard on ourselves, too. The biggest collective gripe seems to lie in the lack of by-the-slice pizza parlors, à la New York City. We are a generally well-traveled bunch. We've seen, we've heard, we know. Perhaps that's what prompted one commenter to wistfully ask, "Why can't anyone just make a grab-from-under-the-warmers, greasy, on-the-go three-dollar slice. Eh?"

Lucky for us, this big group of dogmatic pizza whiners, there are a number of spots routinely raved about. I haven't witnessed a negative word spoken about Dante Ristorante Pizzeria, occupying a slightly upscale strip mall storefront in the Shops of Legacy near 168th and Center. Its authentic Neapolitan-style pie consistently earns proclamations along the lines of "just amazing," "excellent" and "the best I've had...*anywhere*." The term

Bronco's Restaurant at night, Leavenworth Street. *Photo by Jon Hustead.*

The canning line at Brickway Brewery & Distillery, Omaha's first combination brewery/distillery since before Prohibition. *Photo by Alexander Rock.*

Bolognese Bianco at Avoli Osteria. *Author's collection.*

Perhaps Dinker's most famous dish, the Haystack Burger. *Author's collection.*

Fresh slice of Margherita pie at Noli's Pizzeria in the Blackstone District. *Author's collection.*

Tacos from Mula Mexican Restaurant in the Blackstone District. *Author's collection.*

Gelato from Avoli Osteria. *Author's collection.*

Rolled tacos from Mula. *Author's collection.*

A Jim's Rib Haven half rack of ribs dinner. *Author's collection.*

Bean and cheese pupusa from La Choza, Twenty-fifth and Q Streets. *Author's collection.*

Kitchen Table owners Colin and Jessica Duggan. *Photo by Alexander Rock.*

The luminous old-school signage from Piccolo Pete's. *Author's collection.*

The Omaha Press Club's version of the Reuben sandwich. *Author's collection.*

Enjoying the main bar at O'Leaver's Pub with a few regulars. *Author's collection.*

Chef Steve Villamonte's Thunderbird Salad from the Omaha Press Club. *Author's collection.*

Craft cocktail at the Berry & Rye.
Photo by Dillon Gitano.

Right: Hardworking, hard-partying bar staff at House of Loom. *Photo by Dillon Gitano.*

Below: Robert Tim Peffer, owner of Sgt. Peffer's Cafe Italiano. *Photo by Alexander Rock.*

Above: Co-owners Jeannie Ohira and Joe Pittack making ice cream at Ted & Wally's. *Photo by Alexander Rock.*

Left: Dario Schicke of Dario's Brasserie and Avoli Osteria. *Photo by Colin Conces.*

Prosciutto slicing at Avoli Osteria. *Author's collection.*

Anthony Piccolo's Mobile Venue, one of many Omaha food trucks, serving up Italian cuisine at Junkstock. *Author's collection.*

Chef Jessica Joyce of Block 16 photographs the daily special. *Author's collection.*

Sgt. Peffer's. *Photo by Alexander Rock.*

Pho from Saigon Surface. *Author's collection.*

Rhizosphere Farm stand at the Aksarben Village Farmers Market. *Author's collection.*

Bacon and egg Rounders with Hollandaise sauce at Localmotive Food Truck. *Author's collection.*

Fresh berry tart from Delice European Bakery in Midtown Crossing. *Photo by Jon Hustead.*

Wenninghoff Farms. *Author's collection.*

Wenninghoff Farms' first produce of the season. *Author's collection.*

Truck Farm Omaha at the Florence Mill Farmers' Market. *Author's collection.*

Cream of the Crop produce stand. *Author's collection.*

The best view of the Old Market Farmers Market. *Photo by Mark Swanson.*

"authentic" carries significant weight here: Dante is certified in the traditions of Neapolitan pizza making by the worldwide authority, the Associazione Verace Pizza Napoletana.[49] Membership is controlled by strict standards at every step in the pizza making process, from training to ingredients to equipment.[50] Chef Nick Strawhecker earned the proper certification through training at Pizza Antica in Los Angeles. Afterward, the restaurant went through a stringent certification process as well. The big deal here is the wood-fire pizza oven; Dante has the only one in Nebraska. Nick explained that learning the ropes of wood-fire pizza cooking doesn't happen overnight, with staff training sometimes stretching into a months-long process. But at the end of the day, "Italy says we're legit," he declared.

Nick is extremely passionate about each of the many farms his restaurant helps support and can pinpoint exactly where his flour (and every other ingredient) comes from. He makes a concerted effort to use fresh, locally sourced ingredients wherever possible and takes this opportunity to offer a thoughtful, well-executed menu extending far beyond pizza fare. And it's definitely caught on: the restaurant's bustling, big-city vibe pushes into the arena of recommended reservations and destination dining—a far cry from Manhattan's three-dollar-slice joints, but it'll do.

Pitch Pizzeria is another Omaha sweetheart. Since opening in 2009, there have been murmurs about whether founder Willy Theisen—who was also largely responsible for the franchisement of Godfather's—would take such a trendy, well-reviewed concept down a similar path. In 2015, the second Pitch location opened to much fanfare, but aside from that, it would seem the chain mentality is waning. After all, a full half of respondents claim that they only order from chain pizza restaurants when they're desperate.

About 55 percent of Omahans prefer dining in instead of carryout or delivery options; this could simply be because there isn't an unlimited supply of viable carryout or delivery options. Or it could be because we really enjoy making an event out of pizza eating. Recall the persistent adage among us, one that is at once defeatist and proud. It states that Omaha's unusually high number of great restaurants is a byproduct of having nothing else to do here but go out to eat. I would say that's only partially true. There's certainly plenty to do, but we do choose to stay very engaged and loyal with our eateries, in particular those that serve pizza.

Today, we are keeping our mom and pop places happily in business, and we're also accepting some new favorites into our lives. There are classics like the love-it-or-hate-it Big Fred's, the stalwart that is Johnny Sortino's, the extraordinarily busy Mama's Pizza, the impeccable experience at Pizza

NICK STRAWHECKER/DANTE PIZZERIA
• • • • • RICOTTA • • • • •

✓ **4 cups whole milk**   ✓ **1 cup heavy cream**   ✓ **1 cup half and half**

✓ **2 cups buttermilk**   ✓ **2 lemons, juice and zest**   ✓ **1 tablespoon white balsamic vinegar**

✓ **2 tablespoons extra virgin olive oil**   ✓ **1/4 cup shredded grana padano**

✓ **Salt and pepper to taste**

1) Combine milk, cream, and half and half in large pot over medium-high heat.

2) Bring mixture up to 185 F degrees.

3) Add buttermilk, lemon juice, and vinegar.

4) Leave mixture on low-medium heat for 5 minutes until it reaches 170 F degrees.

5) Strain cheese curds through strainer lined with cheesecloth.

6) Leave curds in strainer overnight or until firm.

7) Transfer to large bowl and fold in lemon zest, grana, and olive oil. Season to taste with salt and pepper.

Seasonal serving suggestion: local honey comb and fresh bread.

King in Council Bluffs and the diehard fandom of Sgt. Peffer's. The list goes on and on and on. Strongholds like Frank's and Zio's and Don Carmelo's continue to duke it out over who's got the best New York–style pie, with newbies entering the scene all the time. Brick Oven does a very respectable version cooked directly "on the bricks," and Noli's Pizzeria in the Blackstone

District took the city by storm when it introduced its exceptional crust recipe to the world in 2015. What matters here is that owner and pizza creator Joel Marsh spent a long time perfecting the crust, examining every detail, right down to the mineral content in the water.[51] Only then was the prize primed for consumption. I found myself thinking of Noli's as I sat with the pizza fanatic kid eating mediocre Manhattan pie. *Maybe it's possible for pizza to be a way of life in Omaha, too*, I thought.

This idea of perfection, of stoking a recipe until it's just right, is yet another practice adopted from the forefathers of Omaha pizza. Joe Patane didn't perfect his famous La Casa recipe in a day, after all. And so the wise saying goes: without a good crust, you've got nothing. Add in a real passion for what you're serving—instead of just the revenue you're chasing—and you've got everything. Even the most argumentative pizza fans can agree with that one.

Chapter 4

THE REUBEN AND OTHER
THINGS WE OWN

It was 1954 when Swanson debuted the TV Dinner. The idea of selling a complete frozen meal had been done before, but never with such astute marketing prowess. It was the boys back at Swanson's headquarters in Omaha who tapped into the American psyche and aligned their product with televisions, everyone's favorite gadget at the time. The shape of the dinner was even modeled after that of a TV. And that is why instead of considering Omaha the birthplace of portioned out, processed foodstuff that only relieves your hunger for about an hour, I prefer to think of it as a hotbed of ad world creativity, the thought leaders of the time. Madison Avenue could have learned a thing or two.[52] Everything Omaha is known for has the potential to be contorted into something equally as sexy. Just you watch.

THE BLACKSTONE HOTEL

Knee-length skirts, cardigans and wedge heels. Slacks, ties and fuzzy sweater vests. A sea of neatly curled heads of hair bopping along, seventeen-year-old gals arm in arm with their respective beaus. Such was the sight as a Central High School dance let out on a typical Friday night in 1944. It was 10:30 p.m., and while the night was still young, many raced against the clock to cram in one more stop before their parents demanded them home at midnight. Driven by a thirst for a tall bottle of Coca-Cola and a resistance to calling it a night, they headed in droves to a spot up the hill, the usual.

The Blackstone Hotel's Golden Spur coffee house welcomed them for the customary round of French fried potatoes and soda pops. A few couples split hamburgers. The smartest young ladies would use the restaurant's phone to call their parents at 11:55 p.m. with the news that their table had just been

A 1934 menu from the Golden Spur coffee shop in the Blackstone Hotel. *Courtesy of Lou Marcuzzo.*

served their meal and, out of respect for their dining companions, request a curfew extension, although in truth their fries had long been served and gobbled up. It was less about the cuisine and all about the ritual.[53]

Having waited on tons of raucous teenagers myself, I can only assume the waitstaff was less than enthused to receive such a large group of patrons yielding such a low profit, but since it was the '40s and everyone naturally had a more pleasant disposition, they would never have showed it. Besides, I'm assured by at least one original high school–aged Blackstone dweller that they were always on their best behavior.[54]

Omaha's place to see and be seen as a teen also served that purpose for the parents of said teens, except the main attraction wasn't the Golden Spur but rather the more upscale Orleans Room, located on the second floor of the same building. Those who experienced the opulence of this dining room still long for the days when dining out was an event instead of merely a feeding time. Back then, the Blackstone delivered the most memorable experience around.

Case in point: at the Orleans Room, virtually every dish was prepared tableside. As eggs were cracked for the famous Caesar salads, steaks were flambéed skillfully right next to you. One diner recalled a flyaway spark from her steak Diane falling toward the restaurant's carpeted floors, where it was squashed instantly by the debonair chef.[55] Due to the spectacle of dinner made at the table, the average turnaround time was at least two hours. It was really the crème de la crème of dining in that era. Young parents, in lieu of getting a sitter, would often bring their children, who would be considered eerily well behaved by today's standards.[56] In the days before crayons at the table, young Timmy would endure the lengthy meal and try to tune out his parents' grown-up conversations, which were enlivened by three gimlets each.

Indeed, the Blackstone Hotel's dining rooms were a place where all kinds of memories were made, the location to celebrate special occasions or simply enjoy a night out. Regulars recall being seated by the maître d', a distinguished man who remembered everyone's name, while he was known simply as "the Governor."[57] They describe the ornate fixtures, the manicured plant life and the dramatic lighting.[58]

One thing most Blackstone-goers don't actually remember is the time they tasted their first Reuben sandwich. Instead of a knock-your-socks-off, life-changing moment, most simply accept the Reuben as a continuous presence, a mainstay in the cuisine of the time and a moderately priced offering, coming in at forty cents in 1934. It should have been a bigger deal—but

"Tasty-Pastry" Sandwiches
Toasted 5c Extra

Roast Pork	20	Reuben Sandwich	40
Swiss, Ham (Open)	...35	Chicken and Tomato	..45
American Cheese	15	Chicken Salad	25
Imported Swiss	25	Tenderloin Steak	55
Tunafish	20	Sliced Chicken	35
Salmon Salad	20	Sliced Turkey	35
Olive and Nut	20	Baked Ham	20
Bacon	20	Smoked Tongue	20
Hamburger on Bun	...25	Minced Ham	15
Salami	20	Fried Egg	15
Liverwurst	20	Hot Roast Beef	45
Deviled Egg	15	Denver	25
Imported Sardines	...20	Corned Beef	20

Chicken Shortcake on Smithfield's Deviled Ham...60
Peanut Butter 15; with Jelly 20
Open Toasted Cheese 25; with Bacon............35
Cream Cheese on Nut Bread....................15
Lettuce, Tomato 15; with Bacon................30
Sliced Egg 15; with Tomato and Green Pepper....25
Blackstone Toasted Halves....................25
Ham or Bacon and Egg........................25

In 1934, the Reuben cost forty cents. *Courtesy of Lou Marcuzzo.*

wasn't at the time—that the Reuben was first invented right within the very walls of the Blackstone Hotel.

Common sense dictates that the Reuben is just a sandwich, and it may be challenging at first to identify exactly where it lies in the lineup of "Important Gastronomic Creations of the Twentieth Century." The answer is that in addition to being one of the finest comfort foods ever to hit café menus nationwide—featuring an unparalleled harmony of salty, fatty and tangy flavors—a level of vigor is added when one learns of the story of its origin. Or rather, stor*ies*—that's right, there are several. So if the Reuben is, in fact, "just a sandwich," then please tell me why the conflicting reports of when and where it first surfaced are fiercely disputed to this day. Come to think of it, the Reuben might just be the most important sandwich of the century.

BIGGER THAN BEEF

THE ALMIGHTY REUBEN

Midtown Manhattan, New York City, 1914: An actress bursts into a local deli, declaring she's famished, and requests the shop owner fix her something sizable. So, he grabs the nearest meats—roast beef, turkey, ham—and piles them on rye bread. He adds coleslaw, Swiss cheese and Russian dressing. Legend has it that the sandwich is so delicious the actress consumes every last morsel of the monstrously large thing. The surly deli owner, a German immigrant named Arnold Reuben, founder of Reuben's Restaurant and Delicatessen, proclaimed that he would call the sandwich the "Reuben's Special."[59]

Popular belief holds that this was the beginning of the Reuben as we know it, but let's not become too enamored of the Broadway lights and the behind-the-scenes glitz and glamour of old-timey New York actresses feeding themselves. For it's important to point out that the ingredients here do not make an actual Reuben. Everyone knows that the real Reuben comes with corned beef, sauerkraut, Thousand Island dressing and Swiss cheese on rye, preferably grilled. Using this evidence, one can deduce that the sandwich constructed on that night was nothing more than a well-assembled kitchen sink of ingredients. There's no doubt it was tasty, but it just wasn't a Reuben.

Fast-forward a few years, to around 1928. Picture a buffet table, draped with lavish linens and decked out with shiny silver serving ware. The trays are topped with neatly folded sliced meats, delicately stacked on one another. Ample fixins—sliced tomatoes, onions and cheese—adorn the table, along with accoutrements such as sliced radishes, celery, gherkins and hard-boiled eggs. The bread—a dark, fresh rye—is recently sliced. It's really quite the spread.

This was a common sight on Sunday evenings at the Blackstone, where men did manly things like play poker and fix themselves sandwiches in between hands. Sometimes they forewent the spread, opting instead for room service. On this night, the hotel owner called down to the kitchen and requested something in honor of one of his regular players, a grocer by profession known for stocking sauerkraut by the barrel in his store. Meanwhile, the chef had recently returned from training in Switzerland and was eager to flex his culinary muscles. He drained the kraut and mixed it with Thousand Island dressing. He added a few slices of Swiss and lightly grilled the thing, sending it upstairs with a sliced kosher dill pickle, a rose radish and potato chips. The chef was Bernard Schimmel, son of hotel owner Charles Schimmel, and the man in the sauerkraut business was Reuben Kulakovsky.[60] *Boom.*

The sandwich was well received and made its way onto the lunch menu within a few years. And then it appeared on the menus of Schimmel's sister hotels in Lincoln, in St. Louis and in Galesburg, Illinois.[61] Years went by, and Omahans ate Reubens all the time at the Blackstone: teenagers after the prom, businessmen out for a luncheon and everyone in between. In 1956, a Blackstone Hotel waitress named Fern Snyder got zealous and entered the sandwich into the National Sandwich Idea Contest—of course, it won.[62] Almost immediately, the Reuben started popping up on menus far and wide. The sandwich was getting its due, and everyone wanted a piece of the credit. Suddenly the Schimmels had to defend their invention, digging up quarter-century-old menus to substantiate their claim. It's perfectly fine, though, because loads of patrons remember enjoying the sandwich long before it achieved national fame.[63] Thus, the Reuben is and will always be something Omaha owns.

The truth is that slapping together a decent Reuben can be harder than it sounds. The meat must be trimmed—not too fatty nor too lean—and as mentioned before, the kraut has to be totally drained (no one likes a soggy sandwich). Butter—never margarine—should be used, just enough to toast the bread in a pan, and it needs to be served the moment the cheese starts to gently ooze out of the sides. One place known for getting it right is the Crescent Moon Ale House, where the aroma of simmering corned beef wafts through the restaurant every other day or so as cooks prepare the meat from scratch. The Crescent Moon, known as "Omaha's Original Alehouse," has been around since the early '90s. It began as an unassuming tribute to regional beers and ales, one of the first places in town to partake in a microbrew and good, solid pub food. As it is located directly across the street, many of its first patrons were likely also patrons of the Blackstone, which closed its doors rather abruptly in 1976 and has since been utilized as offices.

It's most certainly the proximity to the site of invention that has driven the Crescent Moon staff members to take special care with their Reuben. The dark pumpernickel rye encases some of the best, most tender corned beef around—no cold slimy stuff here. The dive-bar-meets-beer-hall atmosphere couldn't be further from the elegance of the Blackstone, but the devotion to carrying on tradition rings clear. The bar/restaurant even throws an annual Reubenfest during which patrons can order items like Reuben pizza and Reuben quesadilla, just for the heck of it.[64] In 2013, representatives from Frank's Kraut, along with then mayor of Omaha Jim Suttle, officially declared Omaha the birthplace of the Reuben at a reception held at the Moon, as locals call it.[65]

Today, the area stretching from Thirty-sixth to Forty-second Streets on Farnam is known as the Blackstone District. The mid-2010s saw a rush of new openings, including our pals at Noli's Pizzeria, a fabulous dine-in Mexican spot called Mula, a lounge with late-night food known as Nite Owl, two new breweries, several retail stores and a wine bar. It's rumored that the Blackstone District, which sat dormant for many years, is now fresh out of any new storefront space. Friday nights on this stretch are abuzz with diners, drinkers and shoppers. It's becoming the place to see and be seen again, not unlike the Blackstone Hotel that once dominated the area.

The Best Ice Cream Parlor Ever, According to Me

Legend has it that there was a second very important invention at the Blackstone Hotel around the same time. Butter Brickle, the toffee-flavored ice cream with toffee bits in it, was reportedly debuted to the world from the kitchens of the Blackstone in the mid-1920s. However, try as I might, I ran

Hand-painted brick signage is making a comeback in the Blackstone District. *Author's collection.*

into some dead ends tracking down the exact story from anyone still alive today. A U.S. trademark search turns up the first use of "Butter Brickle" in 1924, and the first registration in 1928 by Council Bluffs candy manufacturer John G. Woodward & Co. Inc. but this is only for the butterscotch-inspired candy, not the actual ice cream. My search for the inside scoop eventually led me to one of Omaha's from-scratch creameries, Ted & Wally's, where co-owners Joe Pittack and Jeannie Ohira were already familiar with the factoid that Butter Brickle was invented at the Blackstone. They even disclosed that whenever Ted & Wally's runs a print advertisement, it features an illustration of the famed flavor as a subtle tribute.

Those hot on the trail for an authentic Butter Brickle can get lucky at Ted & Wally's on select days. There are too many rotating favorites to keep any one flavor on for extended periods—besides vanilla and chocolate, of course. Apart from the classics, Ted & Wally's has been making great strides in innovative ice cream cuisine for quite some time. Pay it a visit, and you'll face the choice of Balsamic Brown Sugar Grapenuts or perhaps Lemongrass Panna Cotta. Or something called Hippy Hog. Don't hesitate to ask what any of the extra-creative flavor names actually are; if they're not written down next to the chalkboard, the staff will pass you a sample served in one of those tiny spoons from across the cooler. And more than one sample, should you be the noncommittal type. This is a neighborhood ice cream joint, after all. You should love what you get.

Jeannie and Joe, the brother-sister team that has been running the place since 2000, tell me they've been able to take increasingly more creative liberties with their recipes over the past few years. The base of their winning approach is an 18 percent butterfat, all-natural recipe. Even classics like vanilla bean—which uses seeds from actual vanilla pods—get special treatment. Skimping isn't really a part of their vocabulary. After all, the ice cream is churned right in the front of the parlor in two large vintage machines, so there's really no way to hide anything.

The pair acquired a distaste for artificial ingredients growing up among co-ops and gardens. Their parents were staunchly against processed foods, so snacks like sugary cereal weren't allowed. Perhaps this is part of the reason why both Jeannie and Joe were drawn to work in an ice cream shop in college. That, and they really enjoyed the essence of the shop. Ted & Wally's, even back then, was a neighborhood favorite in the Old Market. "There were really good people there. I had fallen in love with the business," Jeannie reminisced. Then, in 2000, the original owners decided to retire and put it up for sale. With an earnest desire to not let the shop fall into the wrong hands, they hardly hesitated at taking the plunge and making the purchase. "Some people from out of town wanted to buy it, and I just didn't want it to turn into that. It came down to wanting to keep what was cool about it and improving what you can. We just kind of did what we had to do," Jeannie explained to me matter-of-factly.

Using fresh, locally sourced ingredients was never optional; it's just the way they were taught to do things. As time went on, their commitment to a superior product saw record business with each new season. And with record business came enthusiastic fans. Once, some rather naughty kids threw a brick at another ice cream shop's window across the street. But they were feeding a tension that didn't exist in the least. According to Joe, "We just focus on what we do best—you can actually help each other's business that way."

I picked their brains about where they get their inspiration for the flavors, which are announced daily on social media. It turns out that they've been experimenting with the non-traditional flavors they've become known for from the very beginning. It's only in recent years that the passion flavors have been outselling the standards. "We've always been doing what we want to do—now it just sells better," Jeannie laughed. All of this is not to say the siblings don't have a taste for a little bit of junk food every once in a while, just like the rest of us. Perhaps because it was a no-no growing up, Jeannie has always had a soft spot for Velveeta, which she incorporated into a flavor a few years ago. It created quite a stir on Facebook. While it might've been a bit before its time, we agree that Velveeta still has a chance to become the next bacon.[66]

Let that be a lesson to all of the parents out there who won't let their children eat snack foods and sweets. If you're not careful, your kids could wind up becoming ice cream shop owners—ones who serve Velveeta ice cream, at that. Still, on most days the flavors are a nice balance of the standards and some other, more creative ventures. The Butter Brickle rouses excitement from fans whenever it's on the menu—it's that Blackstone Hotel connection everyone goes crazy for.

REALLY DELICIOUS FAST FOOD (SERIOUSLY)

The triangle is a truly enchanting shape. It holds the key to many of nature's secrets and is the subject of ancient mathematicians' astute, undying observations. Oh, the magic, the sheer energy that the symbol of the triangle can hold. Spinach pie, baklava, the USDA food pyramid. Is there a masonic connection here? I don't know. All I know is I'm holding a triangle-shaped piece of deep-fried grilled cheese between my fingers, and I'm about to take a bite. Gingerly nibbling down, I'm met first with a thick layer of crunchy coating with an almost buttery quality. Then a brief layer of soft white bread, followed by the jackpot: the warm, molten sensation of melted cheese. It's of the orange variety, and if my palate knows a thing or two, I'd say it's American. There's a slight hint of tangy mayonnaise throughout, and the mouthfeel of crunch mixed with cheese goo is really something amazing. Two or three bites and I'm on to the next triangle, of which there are four. I summon Pythagoras, the builders of the Egyptian pyramids and all those lost off the coast of Bermuda. Eating a cheese frenchee is a treat, and I intend to keep the experience pretty existential. I told you before it would be possible to make everything Omaha is known for sound sexy.

The cheese frenchee isn't actually so much sexy as it is, in a word, nostalgic. Every single old-timer I talked to mentioned it. In the '60s and '70s, they used to order them on telephones at the fast-food place called King's Food Host. You'd pick up the phone—every booth had its own—and dictate your order. This really tickled folks' fancy, kind of like an old-school version of having individual iPads at your table. The gimmick really caught on, and there were more than one hundred locations in seventeen states at the height of the King's Food Host mini empire. Today there are none, a very disappointing reality to those who grew up eating there.

The birthplace of King's was in Lincoln, Nebraska, in 1951, but today, the only place to get bona-fide frenchees made for you is in Omaha at Don & Millie's. In fact, it's rumored that the founders of Don & Millie's went so far as to purchase exclusive rights to the King's Food Host recipe. Along with your frenchee, have some fries, onion rings or, heck, even a loaded baked potato. Gee whiz, the cheeseburgers here are pretty good, too. Even a Yelp-following foodie can stand a little Don & Millie's every once in a while. Oh, and they serve ninety-nine-cent margaritas along with dirt-cheap domestic beers—for dine-in only, of course.

It's quite possible that I'm committing food writer self-sabotage by lamenting the value of fast food. Still, I don't want to underestimate the significance of these locally founded, commonly beloved establishments. Take, for example, Bronco's Restaurant, known within the Omaha vernacular as "Bronco Burger." It was founded in 1959, expanded to four locations and eventually downsized to two.[67] Its neon signage on Leavenworth Street, a positively iconic depiction of a cowboy, sports the words, "Serve Yourself and Save," indicative of the fascination with self-service restaurants of that period. The burgers are crave-worthy. It has a pork tenderloin deluxe sandwich that can compete with the best of them and fried chicken that loyalists swear by. And get this: the fries are hand cut. You may think you've moved on with your life, that you have a future filled with farm-fresh, organic produce served over a bed of quinoa and sprouts, and then one day it just hits you: you're hung over, and you need some Bronco Burger. You'd miss it if you moved away from Omaha.

And then there's the other favorite, the legendary item. Picture yourself as a recent college graduate having a bit of separation anxiety about moving away from home. You love the Huskers, but you're thinking about taking that entry-level job in Minneapolis or maybe a bartending gig in Chicago, or perhaps you think you have what it takes to be an actor so you've got New York on the brain. Your parents can't wait for you to leave town so they don't have to feel guilty about turning your old bedroom into the home gym they've always wanted. You're about to go, but there's just one thing holding you back. And that thing is called Runza®. You think to yourself, *Dear God, Self. Get yourself together. You can't change your life for a fast-food menu item!*

The big and beautiful cheese frenchee from Don & Millie's. *Author's collection.*

You can think of it as just a fast-food menu item, or you can recognize that within that savory pastry filled with seasoned ground beef, neon yellow–orange cheese, sautéed onions and cabbage, there is also a massive amount of important world history. Before the Runza® was a registered trademark by the Nebraska-based restaurant of the same name, it was a recipe native to eastern Europe, specifically of the Volga, a group of ethnic Germans living in western Russia. They had settled there in the eighteenth century following an invitation from the Russian monarchy to come take advantage of the farmland there.[68] Later, these German Russians came in large numbers to the American Heartland; once incentivized to move to Russia, they had all but worn out their welcome in a climate of nineteenth-century hyper-nationalism in Europe.[69] Their recipe for the (non-trademarked) runza traveled with them.[70] It was replicated and mass produced when the Everett family opened the first Runza® restaurant in 1949.[71] Today, we think of Runzas® as a game day favorite, but it started off as the fast-food version of what a lot of European Americans grew up eating in the old country. Appropriately, it's often the one thing you will explain to other foreign exchange students on your semester abroad that characterizes "back home" for you. Yes, like the cheese frenchee, the Runza® also originated in Lincoln. However, this concoction—along with a side of hot, crispy crinkle-cut fries and an iced tea—is definitely a major comfort for Omahans, too.

All of these restaurants represent comfort food in its shameless, most brazen glory. A few years ago, I dined at a popular high-end restaurant on January 2, and as I sat at the bar, I overheard the staff recap their respective New Year's Eve hijinks. (As it turns out, service industry workers like to party—who knew?) The chef, who shall remain unnamed, shared that he had gone straight to Bronco Burger immediately upon waking—that the only cure for his throbbing head was the hand-cut fries, being the perfect little grease vessels they are. Luckily, Bronco's was open on the holiday. These fast-food restaurants have clearly captured the hearts of all of us, even our Omaha-famous chefs.

HOUSEHOLD NAMES

There are a ton of other little nuances and tidbits that make up the Omaha food experience. Take, for example, the way we do doughnuts. Everyone everywhere loves doughnuts; for Omaha, it's all about the approach. Since 1983, Donut Stop has taken up residence on South Thirteenth Street, not far from the Bohemian Café. Brightly painted letters on the façade inform the opening hours: an unconventional Tuesday through Saturday until 10:00 a.m.

This is basically the college hangout I wish I'd had. Friends tell me about all-nighters spent studying at these tables, smoking cigarettes before the ban, cheered on by the many cat posters on the walls and a bunch of hot coffee. It's worth noting, too, that the doughnuts are phenomenal. Nothing terribly exciting, no bacon maple or breakfast cereal coatings, but quite delicious all the same. Hal and Marlene Rodgers ran the place until Hal passed away in 2014, and Marlene continued on with some hired help. Other than that, there haven't been many changes. There's the retirees who sit in the mornings and exchange nuggets of wisdom with one another—or at least that's what I suppose they're doing. One recent morning, when one of the men didn't show up as he had every day for years, they sent someone to check on him out of concern. He was fine, it turned out, but that just goes to show how tightknit the place is. It couldn't possibly be a more perfect neighborhood fixture.

There are others that come close with charm but don't quite exceed the mark, at least in terms of atmosphere: Olsen's Bake Shop down on South Tenth Street on the edge of Little Italy also makes great doughnuts, and Pettit's Pastry has one of the finest baked goods selections in town. It was 2013 before Omaha even laid eyes on a Dunkin' Donuts when the first franchise opened, and the Krispy Kremes and other chains are generally pretty sparse. We didn't need the extra boost of America's doughnut. We had our own right here.

Similarly, there is one name that many of us think of when we're looking for a special place to get sausage and other freshly butchered meats. That name is Stoysich. There are multiple locations across the city bearing that title; these are separate businesses founded by a pair of brothers in the late '50s and early '60s. Since then, both businesses, depending on your preference and location, have grown loyal clientele bases that keep Stoysich top of mind for all their meaty needs. For who could forget the big brown building at Twenty-fourth and Bancroft Streets with the sausage-shaped signage? (The last time I was at the downtown Pettit's Pastry location, hooking myself up with a few doughnuts, it was selling savory pastries filled with Stoysich sausages. It doesn't get much more Omaha than that.)

The famous Donut Stop façade on South Thirteenth Street. *Author's collection.*

And then there's the Thunderbird Salad. If you're not a part of Omaha's country club circuit, you might not know this one. The Thunderbird was invented by Chef Luis Villamonte at Happy Hollow in the '60s and has generally not wandered very far from country club menus since then. But those who do know it swear by it. I mean they crave it, hard. Seems a bit dramatic for a salad, but not after you know what goes into it: iceberg and romaine lettuce, chives, chopped bacon, shredded mozzarella cheese, blue cheese crumbles, diced tomato, diced avocado and croutons. Luis's son, Steve, executive director of the Omaha Press Club, told me about all the particulars that make the salad proper at the restaurant on the twenty-second floor of the old First National building. The lettuce must be properly chopped and the ingredients tossed thoroughly. Never, ever even think of using fresh chives, unless you want the flavor balance of the whole thing to be thrown off; freeze-dried is the proper format. The dressing has a secret mix of seventeen spices and herbs and, for this reason, is only available in jarred form from Villamonte's sanctioned production line.[72] Any other attempts without the trademark are faulty and should be avoided—again, unless you want a subpar salad. There is a unity of flavors in the finished product that can't be matched. Track one down next time you're in the mood for a salad that has no place on any low-cal menu—the lettuce is about all it's got going for it in health points. It sure is tasty.

Donut Stop, Stoysich, Thunderbird. All household names in the world of Omaha food, and yet sometimes I feel that we take them for granted. Take a moment to appreciate the folks who've been doing their thing all these years just to fulfill your craving.

• • • • • • TED & WALLY'S • • • • • •
BUTTER BRICKLE ICE CREAM

- ✓ 1 pint heavy cream
- ✓ 1 pint half and half
- ✓ 6 egg yolks
- ✓ Pinch of salt
- ✓ 2 1/2 tablespoons unsalted butter
- ✓ 1 cup light brown sugar

1) Combine heavy cream with half and half in a large saucepan. Cook on medium-high heat for 5 minutes. Don't let it boil over. Remove from heat and let cool for 12 minutes.

2) Beat egg yolks, pinch of salt, softened butter, and brown sugar together in a bowl and then add it to the cream.

3) Heat all the ingredients on medium-low heat, while continually stirring, until the temperature reaches 170 F degrees. Place the pan in an ice bath for about 4 minutes. Then transfer it to the refrigerator for 3 hours.

4) Add the whole mixture to ice cream maker and follow the manufacturer's instructions.

5) When done freezing in machine and ice cream is still soft, stir in about 1 cup or more of crushed Butter Brickle (toffee) bits. Then put mixture back in freezer until completely hardened.

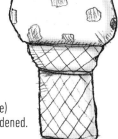

Homemade Butter Brickle Recipe:

(Note: can substitute crushed Heath candy bars if one does not have a candy thermometer)
Mix 1/2 cup light brown sugar, 1/2 cup unsalted butter and 2 tablespoons water in saucepan and cook over medium heat until it reaches 300 F degrees with candy thermometer. Pour it into a silicon baking sheet and let it cool. Once hardened, place it in a bag and crush it.

Chapter 5

OMAHA DRINKS

A Love Letter to Local Booze

It's time to relax. Go ahead and get yourself an adult beverage. You've earned it if you've made it this far. If you're sitting within the Omaha city limits, chances are you're a stone's throw away from some sort of neighborhood pub. Perhaps you're a regular. Or perhaps you've never even been inside for fear of the dreaded needle scratch on the record player and hairy eyeballs from all the regulars. Fear not! Any bar worth its whiskey doesn't treat its patrons any less than awesome. Omaha is full of interesting, off-the-beaten-path watering holes in every neck of the woods. Many of them are fabulous. They are waiting to be discovered by you. The regulars won't mind. Just save them their seats at the bar.

Omaha loves its dive bars. Heck, America loves its dive bars. A dive bar is a place to "belly up"—perhaps until you fall down but hopefully not. It's a place to release the restraints of pretension and enjoy a pint with a pal, or a stranger. Omaha has a lot of these bars. Once a symbol of working-class, blue-collar neighborhoods, they now share that identity with enclaves of well-meaning, interesting hipsters. Dive bars might be gaining popularity these days, but luckily, that doesn't seem to affect their quality. A cheap drink poured under the light of a thousand Budweiser neons, by hands that have weathered years of rough bar towels, is worth more than you'd think.

Bud Olson's Bar, a favorite dive on the Leavenworth strip. *Author's collection.*

A MATCH MADE IN HEAVEN

We've all seen the online clickbait lists that inform us of Omaha's status as such honorable things as "Number One Most Hungover City" and "Second-Highest Number of Dive Bars Per Capita." One might wonder, why does Omaha have so many dive bars? The answer is relatively simple: we've already heard of Omaha's working class that populated the railroad and livestock industries in the nineteenth and twentieth centuries. They needed somewhere to put their feet up, and it probably wasn't going to be the Blackstone Hotel's top-floor ballroom—at least not on a regular basis.

Many of our hardworking immigrant families came from Ireland and Germany. Ladies and gentlemen, we don't have to pretend there aren't generalizations about these populations. Anyone who's ever been to a proper Paddy's Day or actual Oktoberfest knows that the drink is held in high regard. This was no different in Omaha.

Recall Sheelytown, the South Omaha neighborhood that popped up in the shadows of the Sheely Packing Plant in the 1870s. This area, generally thought of as south of Hanscom Park and north of the Union Stockyards, became known as a distinctly working-class, Polish domain. At times, the reputation wasn't very favorable. Lincoln-based historian Jim McKee told of an incident that doesn't seem to be all that isolated:

> *About 1890, the wooden St. Paul's Church building at 29th and Elm streets was purchased by a Roman Catholic congregation, which then hired Polish nationalist Stephen Kaminski as its second minister. When, in 1895, a disagreement arose as to whether the church was owned by the congregation or the church and bishop, Kaminski and his followers simply set fire to the structure and burned it to the ground—end of the argument.*[73]

The area was also "a favorite beginning and ending point for political rallies," proving that all that moxie and might can really work up a thirst. There were even saloons that doubled as banks at one point. Today, there aren't very many visual cues left of the lively and ever-so-slightly seedy neighborhood it once was. There are still, however, the dive bars.

Sheelytown is where I began my somewhat ambitious and decidedly excessive jaunt through seven Omaha bars in one afternoon. The purpose of this, we thought, was to experience as much of the quintessential Omaha dive bar culture as we could in one day. Beyond that, there wasn't too much sturdy reasoning to stand on. We wanted cheap well drinks and a change of scenery. Andy's Bar, near Thirty-fifth and F Streets, provided ample seating, a winning pool table and a thick plastering of sports and beer memorabilia on the walls. There was a very impressive array of snack foods for sale, each package meticulously clipped to one of those chip racks behind the bar. Andy's, an unattached little building on an otherwise residential block where the drinks are stuck on pre-Prohibition prices, is the kind of place that makes you wonder why you'd ever put up with any crap anywhere else. Indeed, your drink is always kept full here.

Onward to Crossbones Bar, a deep South O dive that offers a more in-depth tap selection than the standard "Bud/Bud Lite/Coors/Coors Lite/Miller/Miller Lite/Busch/Busch Lite" drill you hear rattled off at most places. It's at Crossbones where we pondered what actually defines a "dive" bar, what qualities earn a place that title. There are corners on the Internet with loudmouth critics that insist a dive bar can't have that title without being dirty, dangerous or otherwise dingy, seedy or squalid. They say this as if keg lines that haven't been cleaned are some sort of badge of honor. That may be the case elsewhere, but in South Omaha, these bars have been at it a while, and they know that there's nothing cute about sticky floors. Here, the winning trait is simplicity, which these bars condone through and through. The uncomplicated approach to service, drink menu and lively banter is countered by the hyper-busy décor—a typical dive bar will have so little empty space on the walls, covered with posters, neons and other trinkets, that you have to wonder what color the walls really are. There are usually activities other than tying one on: sports watching is most popular, followed by small-time gambling efforts like keno and pickles. They keep you busy so you can get nice and comfortable and put in a real good chunk of time at these places.

On the day of the big tour of all the dive bars, the group wound up at O'Leaver's Pub, a former total dive that's graduated to more of a live music venue in recent years while still managing to retain most of its, shall we say, rugged charm. On most afternoons, the cozy, three-sided bar is populated by regulars spitting out their answers to *Jeopardy* on TV and authoritatively trading their opinions on mostly everything. As night falls, you can find drinkers coming out of every orifice of the place: they could be on the sandy volleyball court across the parking lot, relaxing in the dimly lit sanctum of the rear Tiki Bar, egging one another on with lively conversation on the side patio or basking in the twilight in the beer garden–style courtyard. Co-owner Chris Machmuller broke it down for me, straight up: "We want a complex. We want the O'Leaver's compound." Mach, as he's generally known, is a longtime employee who didn't hesitate to turn his bartender-ship into ownership once this chunk of property occupying the triangle of land where South Saddle Creek Road meets Fiftieth Street came up for sale in 2011. "It's funny," he said of the continual expansion of the bar's services. "I don't know if we always meant it to be this way, but there's truly something for everybody. And as we're evolving, the spirit remains the same—it's just kind of like an 'anything goes' kind of place. There's a freedom to be oneself at O'Leaver's." And he couldn't be more sincere about that.

O'Leaver's is kept thriving by an extremely broad spectrum of patrons now, although it wasn't always necessarily that way. The main building was constructed in 1961 as a bar and has stayed a bar ever since. Mach started going there right when the last owners, Sean Conway and Chris Mello, had just plastered every inch of the walls with records, the kind of thrift store finds you might recall seeing in Dad's collection. I'm continually haunted by Phil Collins's *Face Value* peeping at me from behind the stage area where bands now play. Before that, it was just like a little neighborhood sports bar. "They served chicken wings and had steak night on Thursdays. That sort of thing," Mach told me. Other milestones from O'Leavers' storied past include its time as a "NASCAR bar" and, later, the moment when Dan Leaver's father, one of the former owners, decided to ride the Irish pub wave and stick an *O* on the front of it, to see if it would add to the appeal of the place. It didn't in any measurable way, other than a tinge of absurdity, since there's nothing overtly Irish about the place.

In 2003, the patio saw a major renovation about the same time album covers were being fastened to the walls. The local metalworker assigned to the creation of the fence had remarked that he could do anything custom they wanted with it, even cut out shapes. In the name of "why not?" Mach suggested putting the character names from *Friends* in the panels encircling the patio. To this day, much to the confusion of newcomers, patrons are greeted with six stick figure drawings and the names of Phoebe, Rachel, Monica, Chandler, Joey and Ross cut out of the iron.

As mentioned before, there is a pervasive "anything goes" mentality. In addition to hosting touring and local acts of various levels of popularity, from beginner to big-time, O'Leaver's has sponsored a number of other, less traditional activities. There was the Mr. O'Leaver's Pageant, which resulted in a beautifully shot photographic calendar featuring one contestant for each month. There was the annual Soap Box Derby, an expression of brute creativity and risk-taking that ultimately had to take a pause due to a few good-natured injuries. There's a group hayrack ride in the fall, an annual chili cook-off in December and many, many potlucks and grill outs. "There's not a lot of pretense," Mach told me, which is at the core of what makes the place one of a kind in this universe.

However, there are certainly others who have filled similar shoes throughout the history of Omaha live music bars. A large number of O'Leaver's regulars are displaced 49'r Lounge regulars, a former neighborhood music venue that met its maker in 2010 when CVS decided it wanted the land occupied by the ninety-three-year-old building. It still lives on through the memories, conjuring a mix of the sordid and the splendid. One bar that's still going strong is Brothers Lounge, which has steadily earned the utmost respect of generations of the punk and indie crowd over the last several decades.

Other, non-music venue classics borrow pointers from Omaha's finest dives. There's the "leave no inch of wall uncovered" rule, embraced by places like the Homy Inn, which has been collecting doodads and knickknacks forever as evidenced by the wall displays. The Homy is directly across the street from Sgt. Peffer's original location, and the two have been co-perpetuating the concept of "drunger" (drunk hunger) for decades. Tim Peffer reminisced that throughout the years on any given Friday night, it smells like Romano

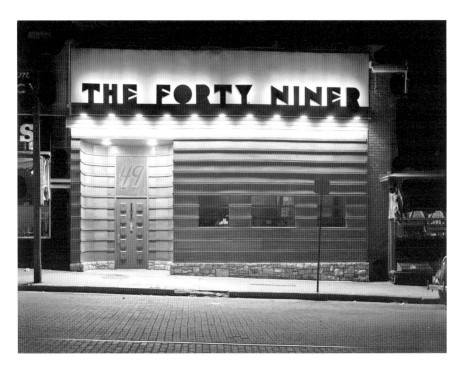

Old, iconic signage at the 49'r Lounge. *Courtesy of Douglas County Historical Society.*

Barry O'Halloran at Barry O's Tavern. *Photo by Alexander Rock.*

cheese in there. The Homy offers champagne on tap, just because it can, and peanuts in the shell served in little dog bowls—just because it can. The absurdity isn't lost on anyone.

And then there are all the other taverns upon saloons upon pubs that are populated every happy hour with throngs of regulars and wanderers alike, both tucked away in neighborhoods and on more populated strips. One such establishment is Barry O's Tavern, an Old Market staple since 1985. A 5:00 p.m. Friday visit will reveal a few neighborhood dudes feeding sizable chunks of their salaries into the jukebox, a group of suits talking shop so loudly it sounds like a shouting match, sports fans waving at the TV screen, an intense game of darts happening in the back, a cast of characters clustered around one end of the bar throwing back their beginning-of-the-weekend shots and, most likely, the owners, Barry and Judy O'Halloran, mingling like proper publicans. It's Omaha drinking at its finest.

THE BIG FOUR (AND MORE)

We've established a few key things so far. One, Omaha's German population dominated any other foreign-born nationality for a whole sixty years beginning in 1880. Two, it's no secret that Germans take beer drinking very seriously. Really, anything having to do with beer at all is regarded with a level of esteem usually reserved for births, weddings and funerals. I am reminded of having dinner at a friend's house in a small town in northwest Germany, where, in addition to massive amounts of delicious, gravy-covered schnitzel, I was subjected to a stern lesson in beer pouring by my friend's father. The issue at hand was the level of foam present, which was on the low side after I had mistakenly tilted my glass too far sideways as I emptied a bottle of Bitburger into it. I was effectively schooled there at the dinner table on how to do it properly and to this day wouldn't dare disrespect a pilsner in that manner ever again.

It's probably correct to assume that your average German population isn't going to feel quite right without having access to copious amounts of beer. And thus, Omaha became home to multiple large-scale breweries before the end of the nineteenth century that largely mirrored the traditional recipes of the German homeland. Three of what became known as the "Big Four" brewers were of German heritage: Krug, Metz and Storz. It was just Willow Springs that was the odd man out, with its main founder hailing from glamorous Ohio.[74] Beyond the Big Four, there were others still. One, Jetter Brewing Company, produced seventy-five thousand barrels of beer annually at its height in 1909.[75] Being one of the smaller breweries, this provides an idea of how large the large ones actually were.

Founded in the early 1860s, Metz Brothers Brewing Company was one of the first in the city. At the time, Omaha was pretty Wild West: streets were unpaved, often covered with a layer of wood to make walking easier. But what facilitated walking hindered any chance at a pleasant experience,

One of the few remnants of Omaha's original breweries, the former Krug Brewery office building at 1213 Jones Street. *Photo by Jon Hustead.*

as trapped beneath the wood was a funky bunch of dead animal parts. This could have been one of the reasons why saloons were generally a twenty-four-hour-a-day affair—a slight buzz at all times would have certainly helped stomach the strong smells of early Omaha.[76] This was also a time when transporting beer and spirits long distances was just starting to become a thing; most products were "locally produced" out of necessity. With the main Metz facility located out of the way near Sixth and Leavenworth, horse-drawn carts would ensure that the beer hall at 510 South Tenth Street was always with a fresh supply of the foamy stuff. I often pass this plot, where there is a newer building today, and imagine what a wonderfully raucous time it would have been back in the 1860s.

Krug Brewery, founded in 1859, was one of the early heavy hitters, growing to a sizable output of about seven hundred barrels per day by 1894, according to James W. Savage and John T. Bell's *History of the City of Omaha*. With this smashing success, it was able to arrange the design of a lovely new brewery complex, which was completed in 1887 at Thirteenth and Jones Streets. This was eventually taken over by Anheuser-Busch, leveraging the convenient location right near the Union Pacific railroad tracks. Today, the office is the only remaining structure of the entire depot, and I've heard people remark that they would chain themselves to this breathtaking Romanesque Revival building if it were ever threatened by the wrecking ball. For now, it's safe on the National Register of Historic Places and remains in use as offices.

In addition to its brewery, Willow Springs had become the third-largest distillery in the country by the 1880s, bringing substantial revenue into the young state of Nebraska.[77] Not to offend any modern-day teetotalers out there, but Prohibition really messed up a lot of things for a lot of people, especially those who had made an honest living out of quenching Omaha's collective thirst. But as we know, people didn't stop drinking. Almost one hundred years after Prohibition began, and threatened many of Omaha's great breweries to the point of extinction, the brewing scene is beginning to come around again.

The Great Brewpub Boom

In 2013, I stood at the end of the Crescent Moon bar in Midtown Omaha. A new keg had just been tapped, and the buzz surrounding this one was drawing more attention than usual: it was the Storz Triumph Lager, the first brew to go by that name in more than forty years. Storz was the sole survivor of Prohibition out of the Big Four, but its product had sadly gone extinct in 1972. On this day, it released what would be its new flagship beer. I swished the first sip on my tongue with purpose and made the kinds of faces normally reserved for weekend wine aficionados at a Napa tasting. You could try to match the archetypal tasting note adjectives to the flavor of the beer—malty bread, balanced yeasts, a hint of hops—but truthfully, this was a pretty basic brew, an American lager if ever there was one.

The brewery—led by cousins John Markel and Tom Markel, relatives of the great Gottlieb Storz—had just revived its production line in a new facility and introduced a brewpub called the Storz Trophy Room to match. The company's reentry into the world of beer making was a throwback to the former glory of Omaha as a true beer town. At the time, however, this restoration had already been in the works for years.

First, Upstream Brewing Company opened in a part of the Old Market that was sort of limping along at the time. It was the early '90s, and there was a lot of work required to undo the pattern of sending all good business to the western edge of town. Owner Brian Magee started by buying what had been the Old Market Firehouse and then the Firehouse Dinner Theater at Eleventh and Jackson, renovating it into a microbrewery in 1996.[78] Today, the two-story restaurant and brewpub gets a ton of traffic and is known for its Firehouse Red Lager, so-named for pretty obvious historical reasons.

Upstream reigned supreme for a while in the craft beer department, and I'm sure it's responsible for weaning at least a few Omahans off of the pale yellow stuff. Then, in 2007, Paul and Kim Kavulak opened Nebraska Brewing Company. I must say that they hit the jackpot with the name, but the timing of the 2008 recession with the business under a year old was less than ideal. They moved quickly to expand their sales outside their brewpub and infiltrated numerous other restaurant and bar taps around town. The brewery's Cardinal Pale Ale quickly became a tap handle favorite. (The Cardinal, by the way, was a bar owned by Paul's grandparents on South Twenty-fourth Street in the 1950s.) A delightfully hoppy brew, it's not unlike an India pale ale, but infinitely more sessionable. And thanks to the Kavulaks' marketing efforts, it had a major hand in putting Nebraska beer back on the map.[79] You can visit their brewpub and production brewery facilities in Papillion and LaVista, respectively.

The momentum was starting to pick up. Lucky Bucket Brewery came out with its Pre-Prohibition Lager in 2009 to much fanfare—another tap taken back from the big brands. Then, starting in 2013, there was something of a chain reaction: Benson Brewery, Infusion Brewing Company, Brickway Brewery & Distillery, Farnam House Brewing Company and Scriptown

Brewery all opened within the span of just over twelve months. While each of these has its own distinct shtick, many share a common focus to produce a well-rounded roster of session beers—that is, beers you can have more than a few of and still be standing. In a time when imperial stouts and Belgian-style tripels dominate much of the craft beer scene, it's refreshing, quite literally, to have your pick of easy-drinking beers you can sit with for an entire afternoon. It suits Omaha's drinking style a bit better than the one-and-done kind of ales.

That's not to say there aren't big and bold styles coming out of Omaha's brewpubs or that they aren't doing anything particularly interesting. According to owner Ryan Miller, Benson Brewery uses a type of ceramic container called an amphora to age some of its specialty beers. Attracted to this ancient fermentation style and the distinctive earthy quality it brings, the brewery had several amphorae produced by local artist Dan Toberer, and it remains one of the only breweries worldwide utilizing this technique. Brickway Brewery & Distillery is unique in that it is the first combination production brewery/distillery in Nebraska since Willow Springs. Its beers, including the highly quaffable pilsner, are the product of brewmaser Zac Triemert's decades of experience, and it seems there is always something new coming out on the rotating specialty drafts. As a bonus, if you visit the tasting room in the Old Market, you'll see the two specially crafted stills making delicious whisky right there before your eyes. Zac has a thing for single-malt scotch as well as American bourbon traditions, and so according to him what you get in the Brickway whisky is a combination of the two styles: double-pot distilled, single-malt grain aged in American charred oak barrels.

But back to the beer. To support all of these new kegs coming out of Omaha, you've got to have ample tap handle space. The Crescent Moon, which originally opened in the '90s to bring in craft beers from around the country, has in recent years opened up more taps to our local brews. Its list has earned accolades from *Draft Magazine* and other national outlets. Krug Park, another *Draft Mag* darling with its fifty taps, also showcases many of the Omaha beers. And Local, which opened in 2015, features one hundred beers that are all, well, local.

There wasn't much in the way of beer festivals a few short years before the brewpub boom, but now there are a bunch to rattle off: Extreme Beer Fest, Omaha Beer Week, Benson Beer Fest and Omaha Beer Fest, to name a few. It sometimes feels like there are too many good, creative beers out there to keep up on. That's not to say that Omahans have abandoned their taste for the Keystone Lights, the PBRs or the "Bud Heavies" out there. They haven't. But there is a very natural progression toward similar styles that are simply done better than what the beer conglomerates can put out, peppered with a growing taste for some more off-the-wall craft recipes. These beer enthusiasts are urging us into a direction of craft-dom from which we will likely not turn back. Unless the United States decides to try out Prohibition again, the Omaha beer scene should be safe.

That's What I Call a Drink

Unless you're on a strictly fast-food diet (and there is *nothing wrong with that*, especially if you're in Omaha, as we learned), it's likely you've encountered a menu where you don't recognize one or more items in the menu descriptions. It happens. Maybe you missed the boat on offal or simply don't feel like pronouncing *charcuterie*. The adventurous order it anyway, the timid stick to what's known and the self-educators reach for their smartphones. The world of craft cocktails can often feel like this. Unless you've taken up a medium-intense habit as "Master of Rare Booze" in your spare time, it's pretty likely that you will come across an ingredient on a drink list that will require some explaining from the bar staff.

Luckily, in true Omaha fashion, ordering from even the stuffiest-sounding drink list becomes an approachable experience. In the early 2010s, as club goers were just starting to understand the beauty of a good Sazerac, a group of enthusiasts opened the brick-and-mortar rendition of what had been years of eclectic parties thrown at different establishments around town. Located in Little Italy, House of Loom is an event space, live music venue and craft cocktail bar co-owned by Ethan Bondelid, Brent Crampton and Jay Kline. Ethan, along with Benjamin Rowe and Susan Bondelid, spearheaded the beverage program, never hesitating in the least to explain exactly what they're doing behind the bar. Ethan told me that despite the recent industry growth and new cocktail menus popping up, the goal here is less about competition and more about educating the community. A night out at House of Loom, where the exquisite bartenders routinely dance while wearing costumes and cranking out quality drinks, will get you a front-seat view into what goes into making these lovely libations. The same eagerness to educate can be said of the Berry & Rye, the bar fully dedicated to the art of the cocktail from Ethan, Brent and Luke Edson. Ask them about the

The Berry & Rye in the Old Market. *Photo by Jon Hustead.*

details, like the reverse-osmosis water system and meticulous ice program. It's all in the name of bringing that one perfect drink to your lips.

That's not to say they won't answer your questions at the Violet Hour in Chicago or Milk & Honey in Manhattan. But we definitely have that approachability factor going for us in Omaha. Craft cocktails blew up in the mid- to late 2000s, when people basically got fed up with pairing their exquisite food with lackluster, overly sweet libations like the '90s abomination the Cosmopolitan. That's the ultra-abridged version. As for the people behind the movement, you can call them drinksmiths, mixologists, bartenders or whatever you'd like. It's less about the title and more about the intent to create beautiful, balanced and interesting drinks that use fresh, inventive ingredients. In Omaha, there's a cast of characters and familiar faces rotating in and out of the city's bars trading secrets and adding to the momentum. At this point, craft cocktail menus are so ubiquitous around town that they're putting the pressure on regular restaurants to up their game. Maybe you're not a full-on bar devoted to the craft like the Berry & Rye, but you can still offer a drink list that adopts some best practices, like squeezing fresh juices and using house-made syrups. Such is the case at Pitch Pizzeria, where the drinks are rotated seasonally based on what's available at the favorite local produce stand, and at J. Coco, which has one of the more interesting craft cocktail lists in town.

The Boiler Room, which is mainly known for Chef Paul Kulik's truly innovative take on Midwest cuisine, was one of the first to introduce a cocktail list worth talking about. It was a ballsy move, considering that the internationally heralded wine cellar takes up substantial space inside the restaurant already. Can you really be good at everything? (At least there aren't any attempts at beer brewing, too.) The answer is, well, yes. The Boiler Room is the first place I ever had a drink with a shaken egg white in it (adds body and texture) and learned what a shrub was (a fruity syrup with vinegar added). On a recent visit, I sat at the bar for an up-close and nosy look at the drink preparation: some required a special shake that seems like it might have been practiced in front of the mirror at least once; some relied on hand-crushed ice, which forced the bartender to hack up a cube with a bar spoon right in front of our eyes; and some, as you can imagine, took up to five minutes to make. It's really a labor of love, with emphasis on the labor. The Boiler Room was the first, and it remains one of the most serious about its details.

But across the board, it's that attention to detail that allows Omaha's craft cocktail scene to stand up to that of other, larger cities. At Pageturners

Lounge, you can get a can of Tecate and a shot of Old Overholt Rye whiskey for a nominal five dollars, or, you can try its Pageturner, a perfectly portioned mix of Old Overholt, Luxardo Maraschino Liqueur, Green Chartreuse and lemon. The Grey Plume's seasonal cocktail list is my personal favorite, with offerings that play up a savory, herbaceous side more than one usually sees. The Berry & Rye maintains the most points for presentation: its drinks often

BRICKWAY DISTILLERY
· · · · · · THE OMAHA MULE · · · · · ·

✓ **Fresh squeezed lime**   ✓ **4 ounces ginger beer**

✓ **1 1/2 ounces Brickway White Whisky**   ✓ **Rocks and lime wedge**

✓ **Copper mug, if available, or Collins glass**

A local spin on the classic cocktail:

1) Add rocks to glass.

2) Add fresh squeezed lime juice to rocks.

3) Add whisky and stir.

4) Top with ginger beer and stir again.

5) Garnish with lime wedge.

Brickway Ginger Beer is sold by the growler at Brickway Brewery & Distillery in the Old Market, subject to availability. Otherwise, Gosling's brand will do!

have a smoke or fire component, or at least some kind of unconventional glassware or garnish.

With the specialized terminology, use of lesser-known liquors and each bartender's unique stance he takes while shaking up a drink, craft cocktails have the potential to be the snobbiest things on the planet. But Omaha works hard to make that not so. Here, it's a friendly effort to bring you the best drink possible. It's a community of bartenders and managers who actually talk to one another and are eager to share the latest shipment of rare imported gin that's come into Nebraska. Most importantly, they want to share the experience with you because knowing what goes into your drink just makes it taste better. All humbleness aside, with the volume and depth of craft cocktail menus popping up in Omaha since 2010, it has become a perfectly reasonable place to go ahead and become that cocktail connoisseur you've always wanted to be. Have the Manhattan of your life at J. Coco, a famous Bloody Mary at Krug Park or a fresh fruit smash when in season at the French Bulldog to go with your, ahem, charcuterie.

Chapter 6

FARM FARE

What Omaha-Grown Tastes Like

Omaha has inherently always been a farm-to-table kind of town. And that's not just for the obvious reasons either, such as being located smack dab in the middle of a bunch of farmland. There's always been a tendency to want to "do it yourself," whether that means starting your own business or going straight to the farmer for your produce instead of through the middle-man distributors. This has a lot to do with Omaha being very good at, and placing a lot of value on, the concept of community. The locavore scene has been strong since before that term even existed, and it gets stronger every day. Omahans seem to get that without community, you have nothing.

BRYCE AT THE BULLDOG

For Bryce Coulton, a native of New Jersey, it was the travel that came along with an extensive military career that really shook things up. After five years in Italy passionately exploring the dining traditions and time taking in the sundry streets of London, Bryce signed up to learn the craft that would signify a new beginning: the art of cured meats (which is actually his preferred terminology over the more formal-sounding "charcuterie"). After training in Ireland at the Ballymaloe Cookery School, he eventually set up shop in Omaha in 2007. It seemed like the proper place to plant some roots, which, after a career that took him all over the world, was exactly what he was looking to do.

Bryce's training continued at the Boiler Room, when it was just fresh and getting off the ground, and afterward to Pitch Pizzeria, likewise a new restaurant at the time. In 2010, he started talking with a few friends in the Dundee neighborhood about a restaurant idea. Anne Cavanaugh and Phil Anania were both from the neighborhood; they were behind the 2009 opening of Amsterdam Falafel & Kabob—in other words, they're the ones responsible for nearly the entire Dundee commercial district smelling of curry late on the weekends. Bryce was especially drawn to the neighborhood, to how it was changing with the addition of new businesses and to the camaraderie and the familiar feel. This is the place, by the way, where you get to know the kids hanging out at the coffee shop, where you know the gas station attendants' work schedules and where the same patrons make their rounds from restaurant to restaurant. (I'm convinced there are at least a few Dundee residents who haven't eaten at home in ten years.) Tightknit is one way to say it.

Soon there were murmurs among the Dundee crowd that a new restaurant would be taking the place of the Subway near Fiftieth and Underwood. I don't think anyone mourned the loss of access to meatball subs; instead, the French Bulldog, as it would be called, was one of the hottest restaurant openings in recent memory. The word was that it would be a European-inspired meats and cheeses place. Rumors immediately began flying that it would be Dundee's version of La Buvette, the iconic Old Market staple that had been around since the '90s, known for its famously inattentive waitstaff, paramount patio dining and distinctive French-style cuisine. I'm happy to report that the French Bulldog has proven itself to be quite unlike anything Omaha has seen before.

The succinct menu includes a rotating selection of meats, cured in-house, and cheeses brought in from both international and local sources. There are sausage platters served hot, a shortlist of sandwiches, a few salads, spreads, quiche and, of course, house-made desserts. The staff has got their multitasking down: the area behind the bar is where most of the dishes are prepared, and your cook might also make your drink. The vibe tends to be convivial and classy at once. A glass-paneled view directly into the curing chamber takes over much of the south wall, and the north wall is floor-to-ceiling glass. Since opening in the fall of 2012, the French Bulldog has lived up to the hype, becoming ensconced into the neighborhood as if it had always been there.

Bryce, acting as chef and co-owner, said that the location has really suited them. He avows that he's dedicated, above all, to exploring the culinary traditions that make this Omaha community unique. Patrons tell him stories, and Bryce relates through his culinary means. Expanding beyond just the flavor as a vehicle for satisfaction, he also takes the scent of food quite seriously—it's a big part of the experience. And so, Bryce started crafting recipes based on stories he was told. He made a smoked Braunschweiger—described to him from someone's grandmother's recipe they ate growing up—in an effort to duplicate that memory. He made a Thai summer sausage in the hopes that it would match the heat and the flavor that two of his regulars told him about. And it happened—he hit those marks.

"Being able to hit that note, to bring that feeling by way of what I've made…" he told me, pausing to think. "I feel like, that's it, I don't have to do anything else today. That's how I measure success. The food becomes an inroad to an experience to somewhere else." Just as listening to a certain record can bring you back to a certain time and place, Bryce strives to make recipes that transport you elsewhere. And with that, the French Bulldog brings Omaha closer to that happy place of being infinitely accessible and truly exciting at the same time.

Slow Food Fast

In my description of what the phrases "farm-to-table" and "locally sourced" mean for Omaha, I am quick to quip that we are not San Francisco, referring mostly to the year-round availability of certain crops in that region or the availability of certain crops at all. (I'm looking at you, avocados.) There's also a higher percentage of restaurants advertising their allegiance to the movement out there. Regardless, there's at least one couple who escaped San Francisco to return to their native Omaha. They brought with them some very sound philosophies on food that are also proving to be pretty popular.

Colin and Jessica Duggan left Omaha to head to the attractive coast, where Colin honed his skills at a series of restaurants. In 2012, they felt that Omaha was ready, and they felt that they were ready, too, for a new restaurant concept downtown. Kitchen Table opened the following year, and today they work with two to three dozen local farms to populate the daily menu based on what's in season.

House-made sodas replace Coke and Pepsi. All of the bread is baked in house from scratch. The seating and décor, mostly made from reclaimed barn wood, is complemented by a large tapestry of foliage and simple flowers on each table. Lunch and dinner services go off with Colin leading the kitchen and Jessica serving food, taking orders at the counter and bussing tables. It's basically a wonderland for those looking to forego the typical downtown selection of greasy spoons. Named one of the best restaurants of 2013 by the *Omaha World-Herald*, the clientele has grown steadily: Jessica tells me that almost half of the day's orders come from regular customers. Their choice to be downtown was largely in order to serve the nearby office buildings—it must be nice to know you're not going to be blamed for any impromptu 3:00 p.m. naps because your food isn't a big ole gut bomb. However, it's not necessarily health food either. Comfort favorites like meatloaf, chicken sandwiches and deviled eggs share menu space with panzanella and kale salad. Extra lean or not, it's simply the stuff that makes you feel good.

Kitchen Table's quick, casual take on farm-to-table is working. I watched as one of the local farmers stopped by with a single bin full of lush lettuce. I asked about the challenges of working with so many individual farms instead of going through a distributor. "We're just here doing what we do, every day," Jessica said. "With us supporting the farmers, that means they can grow more, and that really just benefits everybody." With these guys here doing their thing, making downtown Omaha a better place to eat, I really feel like we finally have one up on San Francisco.

Our Growing City

Every Sunday morning from May to October the summer sun beats down on the Aksarben Village Farmers Market, mocking anyone with even a trace of a hangover. The streets are packed full of dogs, strollers and people young and old. I've wondered many times if it would be possible to feed oneself a full meal just from a few laps around the market, taking advantage of the free samples galore—everything from enchiladas to goat cheese to pork chops. The produce is the main draw, one little sea after another of beautiful colors, fruits and veg of all shapes and sizes. One booth sells the best apples I've ever had in my life. Another is full of stunning heirloom tomatoes. And another has me thinking about what I'm going to do with kohlrabi this week. I've watched the Omaha farmers' markets grow substantially over the years as more and more vendors have joined. Now more than one hundred of them bring their best each Sunday at Aksarben and Saturday at the Old Market.

While these are the best-known places to stock up on your kale for the week, there are others. In Florence in North Omaha, there's a pretty happening Sunday market. Besides your typical beautiful produce and cute crafts for sale, I ran into the Truck Farm there on a recent weekend. This is a mobile education tool that provides resources on growing, cleaning and cooking your food. So if you see a '75 Chevy truck with a bed full of greenery driving around, that's what's going on. It does a lot of in-school workshops with kids, inspiring them to grow their own fresh, healthy food and providing the means to do so. Truck Farm Omaha is modeled after similar concepts in other cities across the country that local filmmakers Dan Susman and Andrew Monbouquette came across while they were making their documentary about urban agriculture called *Growing Cities*. Originally it was going to be a short-term, one-season project to raise awareness and help promote the film, but the idea really caught on. Education director Chelsea Taxman took over the day-to-day operations, and if you see her at the market or out and about educating young folk about the benefits of knowing where their food comes from, be sure to say hi.

Besides the weekly markets, Omahans also have the option of going directly to the source to get their greens. Wenninghoff's has been serving

Owner Karen Kruse at the Cream of the Crop produce stand. *Photo by Alexander Rock.*

its neighbors in the northwest part of town since 1956. Its walk-up produce market is set right on the farm, so enjoy the strikingly lovely sight of cabbage and tomatoes growing when you go. Tomāto Tomäto in southwest Omaha is a similar setup. Both have Community Supported Agriculture (CSA) programs in place to facilitate fresh produce to the people at a reasonable cost.

If you don't want to commit to a CSA, there are plenty of produce stands to visit. One such is Cream of the Crop at 7615 Cass Street. Since 2011, owner Karen Kruse has been working hard to keep her stand stocked all season long with much better versions of what you'd find at the grocery stores. She also makes her own brand of fabulous salsa called Mama Hoots—it's worth a trip to the stand just for that. Pitch Pizzeria's Chris Wray first pointed me here, raving about the cherries he was using for some special craft cocktails. Once you know where to look, there is no shortage of farm-fresh foods available in Omaha. It's what we do with it that makes things interesting.

The Art of Pickling

The rap on the Grey Plume, the champion of farm-to-table dining in Midtown Crossing, is that it doesn't have a walk-in refrigerator. It doesn't need one; the produce and meats are delivered so often, and from so close by, that it isn't necessary to preserve with refrigeration. What may sound like sensationalism at first begins to click when you experience the day's menu, which changes according to what's available. Chef Clayton Chapman simply doesn't want the stuff hanging around too long.

The Grey Plume emerged in 2010 in Midtown Crossing, a neighborhood cultivated from scratch by developers. Attaining a true community feel doesn't happen overnight, and this one's a work in progress. But one huge advantage to this all-new construction was that it could be tailored to the businesses' needs. This was the primo opportunity to aim high and build something that's truly reflective of the values behind it. As a result, Clayton and his business partner, Michael Howe, looked at everything, from the walls and dining room chairs (which are made largely of reclaimed wood) to the appliances (which generally run with the least amount of energy necessary to do the job). All of this extra time, effort and expense toward making the restaurant sustainable earned it the title of "Greenest Restaurant in

America" by the Green Restaurant Association, the clear authority in the field, whose mission is above all to create an environmentally sustainable restaurant industry.[80] Having worked in restaurants for years, I've seen my fair share of perfectly recyclable glass and plastics and unused napkins get chucked straight into the bin destined for the mega landfills many of us pretend don't exist. So I'm sure I'm not the only one who finds it refreshing to watch this movement unfold and contribute to a new type of mindfulness. There's nothing terribly "different" feeling about dining at the Grey Plume. It's just got a calm, just barely provincial vibe.

All of these green construction efforts would be in vain if there wasn't also a matching effort to source ingredients from the local land. And this is done beautifully at the Grey Plume. As is the case with an increasing number of other restaurants in town, the mornings and early afternoons are punctuated by visits from local farmers—in other words, the day's deliveries. A little lettuce here, a little fresh herbs there. Maybe a stop by from Dean Dvorak of Plum Creek Farms, whose poultry operation has gone from relative unknown status in 2010 to the most recognizable brand of naturally raised local chicken in Omaha. And yet Clayton's approach isn't to shove in your face the proud fact that everything you're eating is from nearby. He'll point out the producer of the main ingredient on the menu but often lets the supporting elements shine by their quality instead of inundating the guest's experience with names of various farms. In other words, there's no flaunting going on. Instead of adopting a farm-to-table approach for the sake of calling it that, this is simply the way things are done around here.[81]

And it goes beyond the stunning platters of whole Nebraska trout paired with the season's flavors, an item I'm still thinking about some months after ordering it. It goes beyond a pastrami appetizer that's so tender and flavorful, prepared with such obvious care and attention to detail, that it becomes the sole topic of discussion with your date. What else is there to talk about anyway? Behind the pervasive charm of today's farm-to-table trends, there are real challenges to consider. What happens in the winter, then, when everything is covered in frost? Should we be relegated to the few lingering potatoes in our pantries? It's the less sexy side of locavore eating—the fact that there's real, hard work to be done if you want to stick to this shtick year-round. But Clayton has managed to keep this part attractive, too, by opening a retail space across the street from the restaurant called Provisions by the Grey Plume. In a nutshell, it's devoted to the art of preservation. It begins with a wall-length chest of house-made sausages: dry aged chorizo, red wine garlic salami, fennel salami, kaffir lime salami and pepperoni, to name a few.

Just a small part of the bounty at Provisions by the Grey Plume. *Author's collection.*

These have made appearances on everything from pizzas to cheese plates all over town, and they have a fine place on your snack-at-home roster as well. The scent of freshly roasted coffee beans pervades the western half of the space, and the rest of the walls are lined with row after row of neat little jars of whole grain mustards, coffee bitters, wild plum jam and the like, all meticulously sealed according to the same high standards as if you were doing this at home. Serving and cookware beauties are also on display, the result of partnerships with local wood craftsmen.

This isn't all about an additional source of revenue for the restaurant. It's not like making jams and pickled beets is going to make anyone a millionaire. Above all, it's an exploration of various techniques that have largely fallen to the wayside over the years. Clayton backs that up by offering a lineup of classes open to the public, most of which are taught by the chef himself right inside the Provisions store at a lovely, large wooden table in the back. There's "Sausage Making," "Cast Iron Cookery," "The Art of Pickling" and more. "You have to be personally involved," he told me. "These things aren't meant to be a short process—it does take a lot of energy. But nothing easy is worth doing." This is pure devotion to the art of food and cooking and making Omaha a better place to do these fundamental things.

It was indeed the art of pickling that initially roped in local chef Tim Maides. Growing up in Switzerland, it was the norm to watch his grandmother clip veggies straight from the garden for that meal's salad, an experience that stuck with him as he started growing his own food. Pickling, then, became a natural end result for Tim. "When you grow it yourself," he explained, "you see all the hard work that goes into this produce, and you're much more attached to it, and you want to find ways to enjoy it and save it." An opening on the Grey Plume staff allowed him to hone this experience. "I would come in as early as the pastry chef on some mornings, and I would start boiling the vinegar, prepping all the brines and veggies. I'd do a couple hundred jars a day."

This is just one part of Tim's kitchen experience. After working for years as a dishwasher at España in Benson ("I originally didn't want all the responsibility that comes along with being a chef"), things took an interesting turn when he followed his brother, area chef Benjamin Maides, to Italy for a stint in his upscale hotel kitchen. "That was when I kind of got a little more serious about food," he laughed. Upon returning, he worked at the Grey Plume for several summers, and then the phone rang. It was Tim's friend Nick Bartholomew, inviting him on for a chef position at his new brunch restaurant, Over Easy. Tim's affection for jams and preserves would fit right in. And indeed they did, with patrons still talking about his house-made Pop Tarts. Known for its impressive breakfasts, Over Easy became a new outpost for local eating in West Omaha. The chalkboard list of local producers helped make food sources more top-of-mind than it had previously been for a clientele looking for eggs and bacon. After a move to become head chef at the Twisted Cork, Tim is optimistic about the future of Omaha dining: "It used to be that a restaurant would make its menu, and because people would like it, they'd expect it never to change. But people are starting to trust their chefs more. You're trusting him more now to work with the seasons, which is a lot more fun for everyone. The cooks can have more fun because they're trying new things, and so do the customers."

Tim wants to travel more, but in his mind, it's all about seeing what's up in other places and bringing it back to Omaha. "The community is so receptive here, and they love trying new stuff. They really appreciate it." Whether it's a Berlin-inspired currywurst or a locally sourced throwback to the packaged foods of our youth, chefs like Tim and Clayton, and the trust that they harbor, will keep Omaha interesting for years to come.

LOCAL ON THE GO

David Burr had been working in restaurants for years. As he moved up and started working in some influential kitchens, he grew to love everything about it—the artistry, the fast pace and the reward of making something people truly enjoy. One thing he didn't love, however, is getting off work at midnight and having nowhere to eat because everywhere was closed. Sure, you'd snag a few snacks throughout the night—it was a kitchen, after all. But when you're standing and devouring an overcooked piece of steak or some other equally unservable kitchen error as fast as humanly possible without choking, that doesn't really replace sitting down to your own meal on your own terms. At that hour, if you're not craving a certain fast-food drive-thru with the initials of T.B., you're probably out of luck. So, David decided to take matters into his own hands.

He partnered with two friends of his, Patrick Favara and David Scott, and together they started dreaming up a late-night food option where service industry people would actually want to eat. It had to be something hot and quick because when you get off work at midnight, not only are you tasked with feeding yourself, but you also have just a few short, precious hours of bar drinking left. And it had to be fresh. With their combined kitchen experience, this trio had already developed a strong preference for locally sourced ingredients, and they had some farmers already on deck to help out. Finally, they decided, it had to be hand-held. The concept of street food was near and dear to their hearts through various travels, and yet it was something Omaha hadn't quite committed to yet. After all, Omaha had not been much of a pedestrian town since the big push for suburban expansion. And let's not forget there are a good three months out of the year where unless you've got abnormally thick skin, it's not very comfortable to be outside walking around.

David Scott is an experienced artisan baker, and with access to a sourdough yeast, they started playing around. One day, they decided to cook up some scrambled eggs with a little herbs and a little cheese. They scooped a little bit into a square of the sourdough and then hand-formed the dough around the egg mixture until it resembled a tidy little ball. With a quick bath in the hot deep fryer until browned, these savory treats turned out to be quite delicious. And there you have it. If, some years from now, some godforsaken New Yorker tries to lay claim to the creation of the Rounder, let this serve as the proof. It was born in Omaha.

The hard part wasn't so much coming up with the menu, which includes a variety of Rounder styles, sandwiches and hand-cut frites; it was more about

Localmotive serves year-round. *Photo by Jon Hustead.*

securing a facility. They decided to make this a food truck and try their luck serving late nights in the Old Market (and also Saturdays at the farmers' market). They would call the truck Localmotive and pledge to use as many farm-sourced ingredients as possible. They would make their own bread. They would hand-form every Rounder. They would keep prices reasonable. They would serve the hungry, hungry bar and restaurant staff who leave work every night with empty stomachs because they were too busy on the job. After opening in March 2012, it didn't take long before word had spread. Soon Localmotive had a ton of regulars, mostly neighborhood residents with whom they were on a first-name basis. One guy, a self-professed daily Localmotive diner, would grab some while walking his dog at night. In turn, the dog also became a fan because he would sometimes get little treats, like a wee bit of bacon or a smidge of chicken sandwich. His leash began to pull in the direction of the truck every night.

The truck chugged along successfully until one fateful day in September 2013 when the engine exploded. It was a used vehicle, so it wouldn't have made logical sense to make a costly repair. At that point, it was their patrons who stepped up and showed their support, contributing more than $43,000 for the down payment on a new truck with a Kickstarter campaign, one of Omaha's most successful. Dozens of fans even donated their time to be in the Kickstarter video. Today, Localmotive exists because of the community the owners built it for in the first place. That's how Omaha does locally sourced.

Omaha's Original Farm-to-Table

Localmotive has worked with a lot of local farms to source its ingredients: there's Rhizosphere Farm for much of the produce, Range West for beef, Secluded Farms for eggs, Plum Creek Farms for chicken and more. Other restaurants like Block 16 downtown utilize some of the same relationships and then some: Pin Oak Farms, Branched Oak, Trubridge Farms and the list goes on. It seems pretty easy. You call up your local farmer and ask him what he's got, and he delivers it for you. Right?

Well, it's not quite as straightforward. It used to be that most restaurants would rely on small, local providers for their needs: there was the milkman, the egg guy, the produce dude and so on. A lot of the older restaurant owners will tell you that this was the preferred mode of delivery because you could guarantee quality and freshness. Starting in the late 1960s, larger food distribution companies started gobbling up these local providers. And then the larger companies merged into even larger ones. Sysco, for example, the biggest and perhaps best-known restaurant distributor, started when nine regional distributors became one in 1969.[82] With few exceptions, food deliveries started to come out of one truck. The industry became more and more regulated. Before long, there existed a virtual rift between chef and farmer. Once the two stopped talking, it became extremely difficult to turn back.

As you can imagine, this really put a damper on keeping things extra fresh. Restaurants advertised "from scratch" a lot, but even that virtue saw a decline as more and more frozen foods came off of the trucks and onto menus. By the time Chef Rene Orduña opened Dixie Quicks in 1995, restaurants had been more or less cut off from direct contact with the people actually growing the food. Luckily, Rene had grown up in restaurants: his parents, Dolores and Jose, owned Howard's Charro Café in South Omaha. He knew how it used to be and had a strong preference for it. After launching his career in New York City, he returned to Omaha with now-husband Robert Gilmer, and the pair opened their own restaurant at Fifteenth and Dodge

Rene Orduña of Dixie Quicks. *Photo by Bill Sitzmann.*

Streets. From the beginning, Rene sourced his ingredients locally wherever possible. He was serving Omaha's only southern food dishes at the time and wanted to honor the farm-to-table tradition of the South. The relationships with local farmers started with them coming in for dinner. "I'd ask them to bring me some tomatoes, and they'd start bringing me more and more stuff," he explained, matter-of-factly.

As I was talking to Rene in the restaurant, one of his farmers called with a delivery. Much like at Kitchen Table, this was a single box of lettuce, meant to carry them through the weekend. When you run out, you run out. In fact, for the first nineteen and a half years in business, the Dixie Quicks menu existed solely on a chalkboard, which allowed for changes based on what was fresh that day. It wasn't until they moved to a much larger space just across the river in Council Bluffs that they considered print menus. "People couldn't read the menu from where they were sitting, so we had to start printing them." It was kind of a big deal.

This was the second move for the restaurant, which had been located for a time on Leavenworth Street where Cantoni's used to be and Shucks Fish House is now. Its clientele began largely with downtown business people in need of a decent lunch, but over the years, it expanded to include a bunch of loyal regulars. Rene credited this to his menu staying just edgy enough within the parameters of what the Omaha palate was used to at the time. Staying familiar and approachable was always of utmost importance. "I'd put beef bourguignon on the menu, but I'd call it beef and mushrooms," he explained. Today, Rene feels like he'd need an entire second restaurant if he wanted to add any new menu items. "If I try to take something off this menu, I get people asking, 'Where is that? Why isn't it here?'"

COLIN DUGGAN/KITCHEN TABLE

PEACH BASIL SODA

- ✓ 1 pound fresh peaches, pitted and quartered
- ✓ 4 ounces basil, stems and all
- ✓ 6 cups sugar
- ✓ 6 cups water

1) Bring all to a boil in a large pot (except basil), turn it down and simmer for one hour.

2) Turn off heat, add in basil, stir, and cover.

3) Let come to room temperature, strain, and save peaches for jam, pie, etc.

4) To make soda: 2 ounces of syrup in a glass with ice and add 8–10 ounces of soda water. Stir and enjoy.

Yum!

In 2008, Dixie Quicks, with its mix of Cajun, southern and southwestern cuisine, caught the eye of everyone's favorite bleach blond stallion, Guy Fieri, and his Food Network show, *Diners, Drive-Ins and Dives*. But Rene didn't let that fame get to his head. He told me that the best part about the restaurant business, by far, is the friends you make throughout the years. Eventually, your business becomes your social life, too, and you become addicted to the people. Pair that mentality with the connected art gallery run by Rob that features local and national artists called RNG, and you've got a place that's really special to the community. No wonder it's completely packed every weekend morning for brunch. That, and the chilaquiles dish is amazing.

Although Dixie Quicks doesn't necessarily advertise itself as the bastion of Omaha's locavore scene, it certainly fits the bill. That's how the movement fits Omaha in general: our version is a lot less finicky, less purist, than you might expect. There's less talking and more doing. Instead of a bevy of restaurants advertising a strict food sourcing policy, we use local ingredients without calling it out—it just is what it is.

Chapter 7

DEFINING THE PERFECT PALATE

By now, you've noticed that Omaha is filled with do-ers. Talking about what we are going to do before we actually do it just isn't our style. That's part of the beauty of living in a city that hasn't been done over a million times before. In many ways, it feels as though the slate has been wiped clean. This is a time of building, of determining the identity that will carry the city into the next few decades at least. One thing that's very refreshing is how seldom the Omaha movers and shakers look to what's going on in other cities for validation or purpose. Food trends are great, but it feels as though Omaha is collectively a bit picky about which ones they want to latch on to. Cynics will say that's not on purpose, that it's more likely we're so unsophisticated it takes anything cultural on the coasts ten years to get to Omaha and that some of us actually prefer it that way. I would argue it's more like we're not the first ones to jump on the latest "it" thing. There's a reason why people are invariably embarrassed by their high school photos. If only you'd have adopted a more timeless style, you wouldn't have to be so mortified by your belly shirt and double-zero-gauge earrings. The way things are going in Omaha right now, I'm hopeful that we'll never have to bury our faces at the food equivalent of thinking we were part of the cast of *My So-Called Life*.

BLOCK 16

We are, however, most certainly not oblivious to what's going on elsewhere. Chefs Jessica Joyce Urban and Paul Urban of Block 16 (aka Omaha's culinary power couple) make it a point to escape the throes of their popular restaurant's daily grind and go out of town every once in a while. If they get inspired by what they see and where they dine in other cities, then so be it. Both have extensive culinary backgrounds and come from food-loving families. Jessica grew up in an Italian Canadian family in Ontario, and Paul's grandparents were from Belgium and Germany, as they told me one morning just as they returned from a trip to New York City. Between the two of them, they don't have to look very far for inspiration.

If you had to label it, you could call Block 16 gastropub fare. It has a decent craft beer list, and it's been known to experiment with how it serves its meats. But what the menu reflects is really Paul and Jessica's personalities much more than a predetermined set of characteristics. Their menu centers on sandwiches and other versions of the sandwich, such as empanadas, burritos and biscuits. Their fans plan on seeing an announcement come up on Facebook and Twitter describing the day's special, accompanied by a mouthwatering image. This social media trick, which many restaurants are hip to these days, ensures that they open for business with a line out the door most days. The special generally gets crossed off the board before 1:00 p.m. As such an important part of business, they've kept every single kitchen slip on which they notate the special each day. The result is a bulky stack of paper holding more memories than one can possibly imagine. Jessica let me hold it.

In general, reusing any of these specials is against the rules. Speaking of rules, there aren't many. On the menu is a spicy aioli with green onion and pork rinds over fries with the goofy name of Gangsta Fries, next to the oh-so-elegantly titled Croque Garçon. "We really just have one rule, and that's to make the type of food people want to eat," Paul told me.

It's working for them. That Croque Garçon got some major national attention in 2014 when famous food enthusiast Alton Brown declared it among his top five burgers. "They've turned the hamburger into high art," he wrote. Not bad for a restaurant equipped with what Paul and Jessica consider to be the "smallest kitchen in Omaha." You see, they had been looking for a space for about five years when they came across a storefront called New York Chicken & Gyros in 2011. It was for rent, and they were able to quickly take it over. So quickly that they ran with that name for a while before eventually reintroducing new menu items and rebranding as

Block 16 the following year. The gyro still maintains a spot on their menu, but the kitchen could only be renovated so much. Their staff has perfected a kind of lunchtime rush waltz around one another.

With specials such as the Italian Meatloaf Panini Grilled Cheese Sandwich Thingy, this is a place that's doing really interesting things very well and not taking themselves too seriously. I think I speak for their thousands of diehard fans when I say I hope they never lose that spark.

What It Means to be Omaha-Famous

Omaha is also not immune to the surge of celebrity chef-dom that's swept the nation since the turn of this century. We've got our own, highly recognizable handful of chefs who are serious about putting the city on the culinary map. And if traditional measurements are any indication of success, they're doing a good job at it. Starting in 2008, Omaha saw a sweep of nominations for the James Beard Award, mainly in the Best Chef—Midwest category. Considered one of the highest honors in modern American cuisine, the James Beard semifinalist nominations year after year indicate that, yes, there's an eye on Omaha. The question is whether that's mainly what they're striving for.

First there was Jennifer Coco, then chef at the esteemed Flatiron Café. She's since moved on and opened her own restaurant, J. Coco, in a lovely revamped space that used to be the Wohlner's grocery store. Dario Schicke of Dario's Brasserie, Paul Kulik of the Boiler Room and Jon Seymour of V. Mertz all got the nod, as did Clayton Chapman of the Grey Plume.

Maybe it's because we're not taking them home by the armfuls (yet), but Omaha chefs don't seem to be totally looking to authorities like the James Beard Foundation for validation. The big motivator for area chefs isn't necessarily what people in other cities are saying about them; it's more about what's going on at home. This is highlighted by the amazing spirit of collaboration present today. When some out-of-town guests wanted to hold a private dinner at Block 16, one of first things Paul and Jessica did was get on the phone and start coordinating with other chefs. It was important that the guests got a well-rounded view of Omaha food, and one way that was going to happen was by featuring the work of other chefs: a sausage from the French Bulldog, for example, and a dessert from the all-vegan restaurant Modern Love. The collaboration extends to the producers where the food actually comes from, as well. Nick Strawhecker at Dante Pizzeria starts every Monday morning with a call with Erin from Darlin' Reds CSA. "We chat for forty-five minutes, and she tells me what she has." That, and the many, many other farms Nick works with, is how the Dante menu is formed.

Other restaurants like the Market House and the Boiler Room help contribute to keeping farms busy, which is one reason why it's gotten much more feasible in recent years to support such a model. "I definitely think it's getting easier," Clayton Chapman told me. "It used to be a lot of research and development for us to find farmers and growers, but you're finding that the younger generation of farmers are reaching out to us now and that wasn't the case before. Writing menus this way, putting this business practice in place—it's not the easiest way to do things, but it's becoming easier." As hardworking as many of these chefs and restaurants seem to be, just about everyone recognizes that nothing would be the same if it were not for these farms. "People always talk about how busy we must be with everything, and it's true, we are. But it's nothing compared to what the farmers do. They're the real busy ones," as Nick from Dante poignantly explained.

Many of these chefs are Nebraska natives who have moved away and come back. Clayton is one of these, having spent significant time in Chicago and Europe. Nick also traveled extensively in Europe and worked in Chicago and Philadelphia, among other places. Colin and Jessica from Kitchen Table, of course, have a similar experience. And there are others. Clayton explained his theory to me: "For some reason or another, a lot of us have moved away and spent time in other cities. But we've found our way back home. People naturally have this incredible passion and excitement to elevate their community, where they're from. Now everyone's excited to see Omaha on the map, and the culinary scene is growing. We're all genuinely excited. A high tide raises all boats."

Despite this outlook, there are still others who probably never dreamed they'd wind up in Omaha. But that native Omahan excitement sure can be contagious. One such is Isa Chandra Moskowitz, acclaimed vegan chef and cookbook author, who relocated to Omaha from Brooklyn in 2010.[83] Since 2014, her first restaurant, Modern Love, has been making headlines across the country as one of the finest in the land—regardless of whether it's using animal products, the recipes and execution are rock solid. Isa also draws on a cast of local farmers for her menu, with seasonal fare being at the core of what she does.

All of these chefs and restaurateurs are well known in town for doing what they do first and foremost for the Omaha community. The national recognition follows naturally. Being "Omaha-famous" is, of course, a little bit of a joke, but when a half million or so of your neighbors are behind you cheering you on, it's got to feel pretty nice.

DARIO

At 4:30 p.m. every afternoon, a team of white apron–clad servers gathers in the back of Dario's Brasserie. They've lit the candles, polished the silverware, swept the floors and straightened the table settings. Now, it's time to find out about the evening's special. Sometimes it comes out of the kitchen so they can give it a try—it's always easier to communicate the details to your customers once you've sampled it yourself. They talk about what the best beer and wine pairings would be for the dish, while the bartender cuts lemons and stocks the cooler. They memorize the soup du jour and every cured meat and cheese featured that night. They fight over the best table sections (jokingly, of course) and clarify what times they can expect their reservations to arrive. Back in the kitchen, mussels are being cleaned. Potatoes are being cut into frites. The salad area is stocked, and the meats are portioned. By 5:00 p.m. sharp, the doors open. The lights are dimmed. Showtime. This team is ready to rock another night.

Back in 2006, Dario Schicke had his concept for the restaurant scrupulously locked. It would serve French-inspired cuisine and wine and strictly Belgian beers. Omaha had scarcely seen such a specialized eatery; the idea scared off banks at first. A refusal to carry any domestic beers was rather bold at best and foolish at worst. But Dario was unwavering. In the end, it was his wife Amy's grandmother who helped the business come to fruition through her inheritance, which the pair was able to put up as collateral to secure the rest of the funds.[84] Opening day was December 31, 2006, in the former location of a Godfather's Pizza in the Dundee neighborhood. (That's right: the French Bulldog was a Subway and Dario's was a Godfather's, right across the street from each other. What's it to you?)

In a few short years, Dario's had earned a strong reputation as one of the must-visit restaurants in town. At the dawn of the Yelp age, the user-sourced reviews were pretty much glowing. It was 2010 when the James Beard committee sent its recognition, and by then, other great, new chef-driven spots had opened in town, too. But this was the only one led by a non-native Nebraskan. Dario had been working as a chef at various places in Omaha only since 2002. Hailing from Sarajevo, he had left his hometown at the start of the Bosnian War and, before long, found himself employed at the famed Hofbräuhaus in Munich, Germany. It was there he met Amy, a native of Kearney, Nebraska, who was backpacking in Germany at the time.

The pair eventually moved to New York, where Dario trained in classic French cuisine and ran a creperie. After the 9/11 attacks, they decided to move to Amy's home state to raise their family. Their daughters, Ava and Olivia, became the combination namesake of Dario's second restaurant, Avoli Osteria, also in Dundee, which is modeled after traditional Northern Italian cuisine. There the pastas are not to be missed. Some are made fresh in-house, and some are imported from Italy; all are served cradled in lovely, expertly executed sauces. Cured meats, house-made sausages and *secondi* like grilled steaks and seafood threaten to steal the show from the pasta.

Back at Dario's, the bar is singlehandedly responsible for turning many people on to the merits of a rich St. Bernardus Abt 12 and complex qualities of a Kasteel Tripel. In the kitchen, Dario pioneered the use of *sous vide* in Omaha, serving beef short ribs that had been cooked in vacuum-sealed pouches in a controlled-temperature water bath for thirty-six hours. If that sounds like a mouthful, try explaining it a dozen times per night, as I did. Full disclosure: you could find me behind the bar for a time at Dario's, the culmination of my many years in the restaurant industry. After moving on to pursue what some would consider a more "professional" career, I thought about returning to a side job at a restaurant but couldn't quite find one that paralleled what I was used to. I had been spoiled by satisfied guests and nary an issue with the kitchen. I only reserve the right to gush because I don't work there anymore, and I can tell you that working at a restaurant is not usually nearly as pleasant.

Customers would sometimes tell me that they could recall when the Godfather's Pizza salad bar stood in the same place as the marble-topped bar on which I poured beautiful Trappist ales into their matching glassware. There's a time and a place for chain restaurant pizza, of course. But there's nowhere else in the world that boasts a Belgian beer list and French food menu run by a family with Bosnian and Nebraskan roots. And for that I'm glad to be in Omaha.

The Old Market

I have interviewed countless restaurant owners and managers, called around town to all the well-known authorities and quizzed a bunch of people's parents. One perception that came up over and over is how people stopped hanging out in the east side of Omaha sometime in the '50s and '60s. Those who were here at the time know this to be true. What was once the city's epicenter, with streets lined with produce stands and shops in glorious brick buildings, over time Omaha's Old Market had become much more "old" than "market." These were the same streets where the city's founders once stood and where the very first structures were built.[85]

By the mid-1960s, vendors had largely fallen on hard times and vacated the area; things were pretty sparse.[86] It was a fellow named Sam Mercer, the well-off lover of old buildings, who is credited with having the vision to renovate, redevelop and repopulate these beautiful structures that had largely sat empty. You see, his grandfather had bought up a bunch of land back in Omaha's youngest days in the 1860s; Sam was tasked with managing the properties once his father passed away in 1963. He didn't even live in Omaha, really; after London and Washington, D.C., Paris was his home. At the suggestion of a few local business owners, he began efforts to turn around the bleak path of the Old Market District, building by building. It's a wonderful tale of adaptive reuse.

Mr. Mercer's son and daughter-in-law, Mark and Vera, also got involved. They opened La Buvette in the Old Market in 1991, a dining establishment that has since become sacred to aging Europhiles and young hipsters alike. For who wouldn't love planting oneself leisurely on the covered patio, wine glass of expressly tannic, lip-staining Bordeaux in hand, catching up with old friends while watching people and dogs mill about on the brick-paved streets in front of you. These patio tables become trophies to be won by the lucky on those first few mild days of spring every year.

It was here sitting with Erinn, an Omaha history hobbyist friend, and Julie, another longtime Buvette semi-regular, that we discussed an older Omaha. A dish of hummus, possibly the only one in town worthy of tasting garlic for the rest of the day, and a plate of cheeses with crusty baguette gave us something to do with our hands in between sips of wine. They told me about accompanying their parents to popular restaurants in West Omaha's Regency neighborhood that are now gone. There was a slew of now-extinct chains, a place called Gallagher's and the Sidewalk Café, which was located inside the mall and not on an actual sidewalk.[87] By the '90s, however, the focus had ever-so-slightly begun shifting back east of Seventy-second Street. A hilariously outdated book called *The Omaha Experience* issued by the chamber of commerce in 1990 scarcely mentions anything food-related, but it did note that "the Old Market's shops and restaurants lure tourists to Omaha."

(Just to prove the point of how everyone and their mother had relocated west, even the director of the Joslyn Art Museum at the time marvels in this book at how wonderfully uncomplicated life could be in early '90s Omaha: "I still can't believe that I can leave my home in West Omaha to catch a plane in less than an hour before the plane is due to take off. I think that's very rare.")

Still, the kids were catching on. The hangout spot of note was the ever-blossoming Old Market, which had been steadily acquiring more traffic year after year. "Everyone cool used to hang out down here at that time," Erinn and Julie both told me. It's not the most objective statement ever, but if you can picture gangs of alternative-looking teenagers hanging about Homer's Music and Gifts for entire evenings at a time, you've got the idea. There's substantial overlap here with our friends Jeannie and Joe over at Ted & Wally's Ice Cream; they were working the old location on Howard Street at the time, which they told me was "a little rough around the edges." A block over on Jackson Street, where the shop is today, was pretty much barren.

This constant work in progress headed up by Sam Mercer was first marked by the milestone opening of the French Café in 1969, which went on to provide patrons with forty-two impressive years of fine dining. M's Pub contributed a slightly upscale American dining atmosphere at the central corner of Eleventh and Howard starting in 1973. Today, M's feels like the "comfy jeans" of Omaha dining—you can always count on it to be quite good, but it's not likely to surprise you. And there were others, many more celebrated restaurants that once occupied these quaint storefronts before reaching their maximum potential and calling it quits. And still more, like Ahmad's Persian Cuisine, have been fixtures for decades, rarely changing menus at all and still catering to the steady influx of tourists in town for various Omaha-hosted functions like the College World Series.

The *Wall Street Journal* food critic Raymond Sokolov remarked in a 2009 piece that the area is "a spitting image of other rehabbed urban market centers with asphyxiating handmade soaps and loose-fitting garments."[88] I'm surprised he didn't mention the number of dueling buskers on nearly every street corner in the summertime. Typical or not, today the Old Market holds its own as a culinary destination, and this is still largely the Mercers' vision at work. There's V. Mertz, so named after Vera, long considered one of the finest restaurants in town. It sits within the Passageway, a subterranean retail area constructed in the space of former produce warehouses and topped with skylights.[89] The Mercer family took things a step further in 2009 when they completely gutted and renovated what was once the boiler room of one of the nearby buildings and called it the Boiler Room. They enlisted Paul Kulik, then chef at La Buvette, to make the menu sing with the kind of compelling, locally focused gastronomy that can truly rival the big boys on the coasts. This kitchen, which happens to stand in full, open view of diners' immersed gazes, has helped prime a number of Omaha's favorite chefs today: Bryce Coulton of the French Bulldog, for example, and Jose Dionicio of Taita. In chef world, it's almost a rite of passage to journey through here on your way to your own pursuits. In my opinion, the quaint-meets-industrial vibe of the room is best enjoyed with a plate of artfully prepared pork in front of you, with accompaniments that match the season's textures and flavors.

Paul also heads up Le Bouillon in the old French Café space. It's an ode to French-themed comfort food, with a range of raw oysters, one heck of a satisfying white bean cassoulet and more. The European flair feels right at home, but not to worry: there are still plenty of standard pubs and otherwise unremarkable sandwich places to round out the area's offerings. Regardless of what changes are made to the restaurant roster from here on out, what's important is that not only did the Mercer family help infuse new life into these buildings at a time when things were bleak, but they also helped bring the neighborhood culinary scene up to speed, to a point of relevancy. I sometimes wonder, if this revitalization had gone down a different path, what out-of-towners would think upon landing at Omaha's nearby airport and driving into town, only to be greeted by some sort of prefabricated shopping center, completely unaware of the attractive bricks that once dominated the aesthetic. Luckily, they're instead met with a flock of specialty eateries that immediately bust any sort of myth that Omaha is a chain restaurant town. And the bricks, well, they live on as possibly the most direct visual evidence of the city's charming history. We are quite proud of them.

Benson, USA

The reputation of this part of town preceded it. That is to say, it was once described to me as the "Brooklyn of Omaha." I'm still not entirely sure if that's accurate, however; much like Brooklyn there is an ongoing pattern of development, including attractive new storefronts and rising rents. Fortunately for the rest of us, there is no special accent.

As with many Omaha neighborhoods, Benson was founded as a satellite outpost before being annexed by the city in the early twentieth century. And yet one thing I noticed at first is the strong sense of allegiance: if you grew up in Benson, you say you're from Benson. And if you grew up in Benson and own property there, you're lucky. Since around 2010, the area has become a hot commodity. There was one point where I hadn't visited the area for about six months, and upon returning, I realized I had missed the openings of easily half a dozen businesses in the span of five blocks.

The growth was quick and buzzworthy. Storefronts that had for years housed mom and pop retail shops like hardware and used bookstores were renovated and replaced by new restaurants and bars. In some ways, it was sad to see the older businesses go, but the architectural character of the buildings was largely maintained; one can assume that there's much more revenue flowing through Benson's streets these days. And beyond the neighborhood prosperity, there's a tightknit quality that is really at the forefront of what defines the area.

One of the first of the newer restaurants to set up shop was Lot 2. Chef Joel Mahr and owner/operators Johanna and Brad Marr had all worked around the Omaha restaurant circuit, eventually teaming up and forming their plan. They're known for approachable, American fare with a focus on local. The *Omaha World-Herald* declared it one of Omaha's best restaurants shortly after opening, and such encouraging words paved the way for others to follow.

Opening just months after Lot 2, Taita was also part of this fast wave of development. Chef Jose Dionicio, a native of Peru, offers sustainable seafood with a Peruvian slant—a concept completely new to Omaha. There's also a sushi menu featuring items you're unlikely to find anywhere else in town. Jose staged at several restaurants throughout Peru before working on the East Coast, most notably in Cape Cod. He referred to his time at Le Bernardin, a popular Midtown Manhattan seafood restaurant, as one of his biggest inspirations. And in Omaha, Jose was part of the core team that helped launch the Boiler Room. You really feel the well-rounded experience of the chef come through here; the vibe winds up feeding that Brooklyn-esque perception pretty well.

In order to serve the freshest fish possible, Jose leverages the contacts made over the years from both coasts. Often working directly with boats, he only serves sustainable fish and creates dishes based on what is the freshest available. This method of bringing in a product from outside the region runs in opposition to the concept of "locally sourced," but if you're going to eat seafood nowhere near an ocean, this is the way to do it.

The Perfect Palate

What makes something uniquely Omaha isn't necessarily the ground beef pizza or the quality steaks or the Reuben sandwiches or anything else. Those things can be made, and made well, pretty much wherever you are. What gives a place its character are the people. Omaha's first round of restaurants, the originals, were special in a lot of ways. While restaurants don't often get to be immortal, the hope is that some of that spirit can live on in the newer places opening today. Perhaps the biggest moral to be learned is the importance of community. We've all seen restaurants fail that should have been successful. In many cases, it was likely that it just didn't listen to the subtle cues. It's not enough to simply show up, renovate a space and offer decent food. As we're learning, you have to really make certain you integrate in the community around you.

These days, Benson at night is a hubbub of foot traffic, with bar crowds spilling onto the street and parking at a premium. It's one of several neighborhood revivals to take place just since 2010—Midtown Crossing, Blackstone District and Little Italy have all followed suit. More are on the horizon.

The Omaha restaurant scene is a story in progress, as any good story should be. It's one of community, history, collaboration and, most importantly,

View inside the stunning King Fong Café, one of Omaha's oldest, most cherished institutions. *Courtesy of Douglas County Historical Society.*

changing tastes. Rene Orduña of Dixie Quicks, whose family has been in the Omaha restaurant business for decades, is cited as an inspiration for many of the chefs with whom I spoke. At the same time, Rene credited this new generation of chefs for allowing him to add menu items that were previously considered too "out there." In his opinion, "people are becoming more open-minded about what they're eating."

· · · · · · · TIM MAIDES · · · · · ·
HOMEMADE PICKLES

First, slice cucumbers into desired shape/thickness. Start layering sliced cucumbers into a container and cover each layer with a tablespoon of salt until all cucumbers are sliced. Let this sit in a fridge overnight.

The next day, prepare the pickle brine by combining the following:

- 4 cups apple cider vinegar
- 2 cups water
- 1/2 cup sugar
- 1 tablespoon crushed red pepper
- 2 tablespoons pickling spice, homemade or store bought
- 8 garlic cloves, gently crushed

Rinse cucumbers and salt off and fill mason jar with cucumber slices and cover with brine. In a couple days, pickles will be ready. This is called a "quick pickle" and will keep in the fridge for several weeks, easily. The salt bath keeps the cucumbers crunchy.

It's no secret that fast-food companies prefer to test out new menu items in cities known for having middle-of-the-road taste. So you can imagine my surprise when I learned in 2013 that Omaha would be one of the lucky cities to try out Taco Bell's breakfast waffle tacos, an oddity that you wouldn't expect to get the stamp of approval from anyone, let alone from your own city. No one wants to admit that their town makes a good fast-food test market; to do so would admit mediocrity, in theory. It means that your city's collective taste has a range that's widely considered "good enough," which is fine as long as you're not trying to be exceptional. But knowing everything else that's going on had me intrigued. How could a city's population be desirable fast-food testers while simultaneously seeing a sharp increase in new, critically acclaimed, locally owned restaurants—not to mention a number of James Beard Award nominations and national press coverage? The answer, I decided, was that Omahans have the perfect palate.

The Omaha appetite by and large represents the American appetite—that much is clear. At the same time, our restaurants are generating enough attention to be considered excellent on a national scale. People are pouring their hearts into this place and have been for some time and it's really paying off. Now, instead of moving to a city that already has everything, this group of restaurants and chefs and patrons that make up the food scene are here making Omaha the great city we want it to be.

NOTES

Introduction

1. Jim Delmont, *Midlands Restaurant Reviews: As Featured in the Omaha World-Herald* (Omaha, NE: World-Herald Enterprises Inc., 1993).
2. Omaha Restaurant Association, "ORA History," http://www.dineoutomaha.com/ordereze/1002/Page.aspx.

Chapter 1

3. David L. Bristow, *A Dirty, Wicked Town: Tales of 19th Century Omaha* (Caldwell, ID: Caxton Press, 2006).
4. J.H. Noteware, *The State of Nebraska, Illustrated by a New and Authentic Map, Accompanied by Some Statements in Answer to the Following Queries: Where Is It? What Is It? What Is It to Become? When Shall These Things Be?* (Lincoln, NE: State Journal Company Print, 1873), 9–12.
5. Carol Crissey Nigrelli, "Our Livestock Legacy," *Omaha Magazine* (June 20, 2013), http://omahamagazine.com/2013/06/our-livestock-legacy.
6. Alfred Sorenson, *History of Omaha from the Pioneer Days to the Present Time* (Omaha, NE: Gibson, Miller & Richardson, 1889), 320.
7. Nigrelli, "Our Livestock Legacy."
8. Ibid.
9. Paul Hammel, "Nebraska Beef Backers Push Special $70 'Beef State' License Plate," *Omaha World-Herald*, May 9, 2014, http://www.omaha.

com/money/nebraska-beef-backers-push-special-beef-state-license-plate/article_d754aac2-ea25-505b-a5fb-74cd29e0fd98.html.

10. Todd Simon (senior vice-president of operations, Omaha Steaks), in discussion with the author, March 2015.

11. Ibid.

12 Sally Kawa and Kari Kawa Harding (co-owners of Johnny's Café), in discussion with the author, February 2015.

13 Ibid.

14. Girish Shambu, "About Schmidt: Is That All There Is?" *Senses of Cinema* (March 2003), http://sensesofcinema.com/2003/feature-articles/about_schmidt.

15. Betsy Andrews, "Here's the Beef," *Saveur*, July 20, 2013, http://www.saveur.com/article/Travels/Omaha-Steakhouses.

16. Susan Szalewski, "Anthony's Steakhouse Founder Tony Fucinaro Dead at 82," *Omaha World-Herald*, July 30, 2015, http://www.omaha.com/news/anthony-s-steakhouse-founder-tony-fucinaro-dead-at/article_828239a8-c20e-5795-a57b-24682a569512.html.

17. Cascio's Steak House, "About Us," http://www.casciossteakhouse.com/ordereze/1001/Page.aspx.

18. Martha Stoddard, "'Beef State' Nebraska License Plates Now Available," *Omaha World-Herald*, June 27, 2014, http://www.omaha.com/news/nebraska/beef-state-nebraska-license-plates-now-available/article_98b2eb52-fe1f-11e3-ab2e-0017a43b2370.html.

Chapter 2

19. Union Pacific, "History," https://www.up.com/aboutup/history/overview/building_road/index.htm.

20. Ibid.

21. Noteware, *State of Nebraska*, 12.

22. Mead & Hunt Inc., "Reconnaissance Survey of Portions of South Omaha," 7, http://www.nebraskahistory.org/histpres/reports/omaha_south.pdf.

23. Lawrence H. Larsen and Barbara J. Cottrell Larson, *The Gate City: A History of Omaha* (Omaha, NE: University of Nebraska Press, 1997).

24. Mead & Hunt Inc. "Reconnaissance Survey of Portions of South Omaha," 5.

25. Harry B. Otis, with Donald H. Erickson, *E Pluribus Omaha: Immigrants All* (Omaha, NE: Lamplighter Press, 2000).

26. Restoration Exchange, "Mission Statement," http://www. restorationexchange.org.

27. Vince Furlong (Restoration Exchange), in discussion with the author, April 2015.

28. Carlos Jacobo, in discussion with the author, April 2012.

29. El Alamo, http://elalamoomaha.com.

30. Dan Scheuerman, "South Omaha Connector Marcos Mora Expands Reach with Latino Productions," *Midlands Business Journal* (October 25, 2013).

31. *Chicago Tribune*, "No Carpin' Here About 'Famous Fish,'" January 14, 1998, http://articles.chicagotribune.com/1998-01-14/news/9801140063_1_carp-fish-famous.

32. Eddie's Catering, "About Us," eddiescatering.com.

33. Jim McKee, "Sheelytown Almost but Never Quite an Actual Town," *Lincoln Journal Star*, September 1, 2013, http://journalstar.com/news/local/jim-mckee-sheelytown-almost-but-never-quite-an-actual-town/article_e5cb961c-174d-5a5f-886c-14274d30efaf.html.

34. Ibid.

35. Mead & Hunt Inc., "Reconnaissance Survey of Portions of South Omaha," 7.

36. Ibid.

37. Fritz Mueller Obituary, *Omaha Daily Bee*, November 5, 1923.

38. Frederick C. Luebke, "The German-American Alliance in Nebraska, 1910–1917," *Nebraska History* 49 (1968): 165–85.

39. Jim Hall (owner of Orsi's Bakery), in discussion with the author, May 2015.

40. Sarah Baker Hansen, "Venice Inn to Close; Omaha to Be without a Caniglia-Named Italian Restaurant for 1st Time in 94 Years," *Omaha World-Herald*, February 19, 2014, http://www.omaha.com/go/venice-inn-to-close-omaha-to-be-without-a-caniglia/article_97734d8a-0f35-5fe8-82d6-206add5b6a3a.html.

41. NPR, "Soul Food for Thanksgiving: Mac and Cheese, 'Red Drink,' and More," November 20, 2013 (accessed July 4, 2015), http://www.npr.org/2013/11/20/246334552/soul-food-mac-and-cheese-red-drink-and-more-for-thanksgiving.

42. Sarah Baker Hansen, "Review: Good Food, Friendly Atmosphere at Big Mama's Sandwich Shop," *Omaha World-Herald*, July 19, 2013 (accessed July 20, 2015), http://www.omaha.com/living/review-good-food-friendly-atmosphere-at-big-mama-s-sandwich/article_7ca5c166-0d6f-54b4-bb4f-b55ad9762fbb.html.

43. Adam Klinker, "Greek Food Still a 'Delight' at John's," *Bellevue Leader*, April 12, 2014 (accessed July 20, 2015), http://www.omaha.com/sarpy/bellevue/greek-food-still-a-delight-at-john-s/article_be6c54f8-0429-550f-8889-6d753b183c51.html.

CHAPTER 3

44. "Pizza in Omaha" was a survey conducted from April 28, 2015, to June 16, 2015, by the author; it had 296 participants from the Omaha metropolitan area.

45. John Mariani, *America Eats Out: An Illustrated History of Restaurants, Taverns, Coffee Shops, Speakeasies, and Other Establishments that Have Fed Us for 350 Years* (New York: William Morrow & Company, 1991), 65.

46. *Omaha World-Herald*, "Caniglia Family's History in Omaha Restaurant Scene Spans Nearly a Century," February 19, 2014, http://www.omaha.com/go/caniglia-family-s-history-in-omaha-restaurant-scene-spans-nearly/article_e7815a44-0f9a-502e-84fa-c9b642dce28f.html.

47. Nicole Jesse and Joel Hahn (co-owners of La Casa Pizzaria), in discussion with the author, April 2015.

48. Robert Tim Peffer (owner of Sgt. Peffer's Cafe Italiano), in discussion with the author, March 2015.

49. Menu, Dante Ristorante Pizzeria, http://dantepizzeria.com.

50. Associazione Verace Pizza Napoletana, "Get Certified," http://americas.pizzanapoletana.org/getcertifed_oven.php.

51. Sarah Baker Hansen, "Dining Review: Blackstone Pizzeria Credits NYC Water for Pies' New York Flavor," *Omaha World-Herald*, June 11, 2015, http://www.omaha.com/go/dining-review-blackstone-pizzeria-credits-nyc-water-for-pies-new/article_2656fdfe-4cef-5cb7-a4e9-b6f848b8459c.html.

CHAPTER 4

52. Robert Klara, "How Swanson's TV Dinners Made It to the Digital Age," *AdWeek* (April 21, 2015), http://www.adweek.com/news/advertising-branding/how-swanson-s-tv-dinners-made-it-digital-age-164127.

53. Lois Anne Headrick (former Blackstone Hotel regular customer), in discussion with the author, Omaha, Nebraska, March 2015.

54. Ibid.

55. Ibid.

56. Ibid.

57. Judy Horan, "Crystal and Corned Beef," *Omaha Magazine* (May 28, 2014).

58. Headrick, in discussion with the author.

59. Craig Claiborne, "Whence the Reuben? Omaha, It Seems," *New York Times*, May 17, 1976.

60. Mary Bernstein (daughter of Blackstone Hotel chef Bernard Schimmel), in discussion with the author, Omaha, Nebraska, March 2015.

61. Ibid.

62. Elizabeth Weil, "My Grandfather Invented the Reuben Sandwich. Right?" *New York Times*, June 7, 2013.

63. Bernstein, in discussion with the author.

64. Sarah Baker Hansen, "ReubenFest Returns to Crescent Moon," *Omaha World-Herald*, November 7, 2013.

65. Sarah Baker Hansen, "Frank's Kraut Officially Declares Omaha 'The Home of the Reuben Sandwich,'" *Omaha World-Herald*, February 28, 2013.

66. Jeannie Ohira and Joe Pittack (owners of Ted & Wally's Ice Cream), in discussion with the author, March 2015.

67. Bronco's Restaurant, "We Are the Original 'Fast Food,'" http://www.broncoburgers.com/ordereze/Content/2/Summary.aspx.

68. David J. Wishart, ed., "German Russians," *Encyclopedia of the Great Plains*, University of Nebraska–Lincoln, http://plainshumanities.unl.edu/encyclopedia/doc/egp.ea.012.

69. Ibid.

70. Tom Isern, "Searching for ethnic food on the Northern Plains," *Germans from Russia Heritage Collection*, North Dakota State University Libraries, https://library.ndsu.edu/grhc/history_culture/custom_traditions/ethnicfood.html.

71. Runza, "About," www.runza.com.

72. Steve Villamonte (executive director of Omaha Press Club), in discussion with the author, May 2015.

CHAPTER 5

73. McKee, "Sheelytown Almost but Never Quite an Actual Town."

74. Jim McKee, "Omaha Was Home to the Third Largest Distiller in Nation," *Lincoln Journal Star*, June 26, 2011, http://journalstar.com/news/local/jim-mckee-omaha-was-home-to-the-third-largest-distiller/article_b1a8ed73-ba56-5b0f-b3f0-46df51cc1656.html.

75. A.C. Jetter (great-great-grand-nephew of brewery founder Balthas Jetter), in discussion with the author, October 2013.

76. Bristow, *A Dirty, Wicked Town*.

77. McKee, "Omaha Was Home to the Third Largest Distiller."

78. Judy Horan, "Fires, Ghosts, and Alligators," *Omaha Magazine* (April 15, 2015), http://omahamagazine.com/2015/04/13795.

79. Nebraska Brewing Company, "About," http://nebraskabrewingco.com/about.

Chapter 6

80. Green Restaurant Association, "About Us," http://dinegreen.com/about-us.asp.
81. Julie Anderson, "A Big Helping of Sustainability: New Midtown Eatery Declared Nation's Greenest," *Omaha World-Herald*, December 9, 2010, http://thegreyplume.com/a-big-helping-of-sustainability.
82. Ulrich Boser, "Every Bite You Take," *Slate Magazine* (February 21, 2007), http://www.slate.com/articles/life/food/2007/02/every_bite_you_take.html.

Chapter 7

83. Chris Wolfgang, "Isa Chandra Moskowitz: Cooks like a Vegan, Jewish Grandma," *Omaha Magazine* (November 4, 2013), http://omahamagazine.com/2013/11/isa-chandra-moskowitz.
84. Amy Schicke (co-owner of Dario's Brasserie), in discussion with the author, August 2015.
85. Bristow, *Dirty, Wicked Town*.
86. Leo Adam Biga, "Sam Mercer: The Old Market's Godfather," *Omaha Magazine* (April 25, 2013), http://omahamagazine.com/2013/04/sam-mercer.
87. Erinn Tighe and Julie Cymbalista, in discussion with the author, April 19, 2015.
88. Raymond Sokolov, "Local Ingredients Are Stars of Omaha's Deft Eateries," *Wall Street Journal*, October 31, 2009, http://www.wsj.com/articles/SB10001424052748704322004574477233569468744.
89. Lainey Seyler, "Prize Acquisition: Veteran Restaurateur David Hayes Takes Over Old Market Institution V. Mertz," *The Encounter* (May/June 2011).

INDEX

ABOUT THE AUTHOR

With a background in history and education, Rachel P. Grace is also a huge fan of cooking—other people's cooking, that is. Her enchantment with the restaurant industry began during her tenure as a diner waitress in high school, and it hasn't let up since.

Moving up into more prestigious dining rooms, Grace developed a deep appreciation for all the dedicated work happening behind the scenes in restaurant kitchens. After more than a decade in the industry, she spent several years existing almost entirely off of German street food before relocating to  the Midwest. Soon after, it became apparent that Omaha has just as much compelling history as that of her native Philadelphia—and a competitive food scene to match. She now spends most of her time finding ways to bring together the things she loves: food, history, writing and helping promote talented people who are doing great things.

Grace's writing has appeared in the *Reader* and *Omahype,* among other outlets, as well as on her blog, "Fat in Omaha." She lives in the Midtown area and works as a writer/producer.

Visit us at
www.historypress.net
....
This title is also available as an e-book